GPCL

Assistant Manager

Latest Edition
Practice Kit

05 Tests
05 Mock Test

Based On Real Exam Pattern

✓ Thoroughly Revised and Updated

✓ Detailed Analysis of all MCQs

Title : GPCL Assistant Manager
Author Name : Mr. Rohit Manglik
Published By : EduGorilla Community Pvt. Ltd.
Publishers Address : 12/651, First Floor Opp. Arvindo Park, Near Jama Masjid, Indira Nagar, Lucknow, Uttar Pradesh-226016, India

Copyright EduGorilla

ISBN : 978-93-90893-77-5
Second Edition

Disclaimer EduGorilla

Compiled and created by EduGorilla Community Pvt. Ltd

Printed By EduGorilla Community Pvt. Ltd.

ROHIT MANGLIK
CEO, EduGorilla

Dear Applicants,

People say *"Success comes to those who work hard."* But I've seen people working hard for their exams day in and day out for marginal success. While others succeed in their examinations by putting in just half the work. So are they God Gifted? No! I believe that it's because they work *smart* and not just *hard*. Similarly, for your exams, you should strategize your preparation so as to increase the likelihood of success. Well with EduGorilla get ready to increase your *chances of selection* in your exam by *16x*.

EduGorilla helps you in not only working *hard* but also working in a *smart and strategic* manner. With EduGorilla's preparation package, you get a chance to make your exam preparation easy, and a fun learning path towards selection. Finding the right path to your preparations can be difficult if you don't know in which direction to head. Don't worry, we have you covered! EduGorilla will be your guide to success in your journey. With our Preparation Package, you can prepare strategically and beat the exam in just one attempt.

EduGorilla's Preparation Package includes-

- **Test Series**
- **Books**

Our preparation package is handcrafted as per the latest changes, expert opinions, and students' discretion. Thus, enabling you to get through each stage of the selection process for your exam.

Our Books are designed by the teachers and experts of the respective exam with a combined 150+ years of experience; to provide you with easy, efficient, and effective learning. Our books are smart, in the sense that not only do they give you the answers to the questions but also provide similar questions for practice.

EduGorilla's competent Test Series gives you real-time experience and confidence through which you can clear your offline or online exam in just one attempt. We currently host 83,000+ mock tests for 1,440+ competitive and academic exams.

Thus, EduGorilla misses no chance to assist you in your preparation and covers all stages of the exam, so that you don't have to look anywhere else.

We provide complete preparation packages for defense, banking, teaching, and other National & State-Level exams. Hence, it doesn't matter which exam you aspire to because you will reach your success.

ALL THE BEST !

Let EduGorilla be your Guide to Success.

Rohit Manglik,
Founder and CEO, EduGorilla

Editor's Note

INTRODUCTION

EduGorilla focuses on guiding students to succeed in their examinations. With that in mind, our book, titled “GPCL : Assistant Manager”, has been drafted through the collective efforts of our distinguished experts with 150+ years of combined experience. This book consists of questions that are created following the latest changes in the syllabus and exam pattern. We compiled the book on the basis of questions that are most likely to appear in the GPCL Assistant Manager. Through EduGorilla's “GPCL : Assistant Manager” your chances of success will increase 16x.

EduGorilla does this through our Complete Preparation Package. This package consists of well-conceptualized and structured content in the form of questions that are tailor-made according to your needs and will help you practice for exams in a smart way by pinpointing all the necessary information. It also provides hints and solutions, along with a smart answer sheet for your self-evaluation. You can assess your shortcomings and work accordingly on areas that may require more of your attention.

EduGorilla promises to help you succeed in your examination and accomplish your dream goals. We believe in our aspirants and see them at the top of the merit list. And the first step towards the top is to start preparing with us. EduGorilla's “GPCL : Assistant Manager” includes the following attributes.

- Well-Researched Content
- Top-Notch Quality
- Detailed Answers and Analysis
- Smart Answer Sheet
- Exam Relevant Questions

Therefore, EduGorilla fortifies your preparation and makes it durable enough to help you stand tall and beat the examination.

GPCL Assistant Manager

Scan QR code for Eligibility, Exam Pattern, Syllabus and more.

Book ID: 0697

TABLE OF CONTENTS

Mock Test 01

General knowledge And Current Affairs

Q.1 Which country won the 2022 U19 Cricket World Cup title?

A. India **B.** England
C. West Indies **D.** Sri Lanka

Q.2 Raja Todar Mal was associated with:

A. Music **B.** Literature
C. Finance **D.** Law

Q.3 The Paithan (Jayakwadi) Hydro-electric project, completed with the help of Japan, is on the river:

A. Ganga **B.** Cauvery
C. Narmada **D.** Godavari

Q.4 Who will give voice to Elsa in the Tamil version of the Hollywood film 'Frozen 2'?

A. Taapsee Pannu **B.** Anushka Shetty
C. Tamannaah **D.** Shruti Haasan

Q.5 The Covid-19 RT-PCR test kits of which Indian company has received validation from Drug Controller of India?

A. MyLab **B.** Swagene
C. Aquitylabs **D.** Pfizer

Q.6 When is the Anti-leprosy day for the year 2020, observed across the world?

A. January 26 **B.** January 27
C. January 28 **D.** January 29

Q.7 Who proposed the Preamble before the Drafting Committee of the Constitution?

A. Jawaharlal Nehru **B.** B. R. Ambedkar
C. B. N. Rau **D.** Mahatma Gandhi

Q.8 A no-confidence motion against the Union Government can be initiated in which among the following?

A. Only Lok Sabha
B. Only Rajya Sabha
C. Either Lok Sabha or Rajya Sabha
D. Only Lok Sabha with the prior consent of President

Q.9 Name the scientist who had discovered that some molecules have mirror images?

A. Lord Kelvin **B.** Louis Pasteur
C. Robert Hooke **D.** Henry Moseley

Q.10 The GST council has decided on a four-tier structure of taxation to cover most goods and services. Which of the following is a correct group of these four tiers?

A. 5%, 10%, 15% and 20%
B. 5%, 12%, 18% and 22%
C. 5%, 12%, 18% and 28%
D. 5%, 13%, 18% and 32%

Mine management, Legislation and General Safety

Q.11 Information that originates outside the organization is known as external information. Which of the following is an example of external information in an organization?

A. Daily receipts and expenditures
B. Salesperson Quotas
C. Descriptions of customer satisfaction with products and services
D. Quantity of an item in hand or in inventory

Q.12 The purpose of job enrichment is to _____

A. expand the number of tasks an individual can do.
B. increase job efficiency.
C. increase job effectiveness.
D. increase job satisfaction in middle management.

Q.13 Strategic planning as a broad concept consists of _____

A. corporate strategy and business strategy.
B. strategy formulation and strategy implementation.
C. inputs and outputs.
D. environmental analysis and internal analysis.

Q.14 Organization structure primarily refers to _______

A. how activities are coordinated & controlled.
B. how resources are allocated.
C. the location of departments and office space.
D. the policy statements developed by the firm.

Q.15 What term is used for the extent to which an individual displays different behaviors in different situations?

A. continuity **B.** integrity
C. flexibility **D.** distinctiveness

Q.16 Critical path method:

A. Helps in ascertaining time schedules.
B. Makes better and detailed planning possible.
C. Provides a standard method for communicating project plans schedules and time and cost performance.
D. All of the above.

Q.17 In Break-Even Analysis, total cost consists of:

A. fixed cost
B. variable cost
C. fixed cost + variable cost
D. fixed cost + variable cost + overheads

Q.18 Investment can be defined:

A. Person's dedication to purchasing a house or flat
B. Use of capital on assets to receive returns
C. Usage of money on the production process of products

and services

D. Net additions made to the nation's capital stocks

Q.19 When was the OSH Act enacted?

A. 1980 **B.** 1930 **C.** 1945 **D.** 1970

Q.20 Purchasing responsibilities can be divided into Buying, Clerical, and ....division.

A. packing **B.** traffic
C. record **D.** follow up

Q.21 Coal mine disasters in West Bengal are due to:

A. slumping **B.** faulting
C. inadequate stowing **D.** flooding

Q.22 PERT analysis is based on:

A. Optimistic time **B.** Pessimistic time
C. Most likely time **D.** All the above

Q.23 Periodical medical examination is carried out for every:

A. 3 years **B.** 5 years **C.** 6 years **D.** 4 years

Q.24 The remuneration for the members of the committee shall be fixed by:

A. Central Govt.
B. State Govt.
C. The mining company
D. None

Q.25 The workmen inspector shall be employed if the number of persons employed exceed:

A. 500 **B.** 1500 **C.** 1000 **D.** 100

Q.26 ____________ hydrogen explosions, known as hydrogen "pops" are fairly common in firefighting.

A. Every **B.** Small
C. Large **D.** None of above

Q.27 High voltage is defined as:

A. a voltage higher than 1,200 volts.
B. a voltage higher than 1,000 volts.
C. a voltage higher than 750 volts.
D. a voltage higher than 660 volts.

Q.28 Runaway switch is used in connection with:

A. direct rope haulage **B.** endless haulage
C. gravity haulage **D.** tail rope haulage

Q.29 Creche is mandatory under the Factories Act where ___________ workers are employed.

A. 40 **B.** 100 **C.** 30 **D.** 250

Q.30 Side Discharge Loader is a:

A. Crawler mounted machine.
B. Tyre mounted machine.
C. Rail-mounted machine.
D. Both A and B.

Q.31 The minimum wages act comes in?

A. 1952 **B.** 1948 **C.** 1947 **D.** 1955

Q.32 The responsibility for the maintenance of employee health and safety is with:

A. employees **B.** employers
C. government **D.** all of the above

Q.33 Ensuring the safety, health and welfare of the employees is the primary purpose of the:

A. Factories Act, 1948
B. Payment of Wages Act, 1936
C. Equal Remuneration Act, 1976
D. Industrial Disputes Act, 1947

Q.34 Risk management is the responsibility of the:

A. customer **B.** investor
C. developer **D.** project team

Q.35 RE represents what?

A. Risk expense **B.** Related expense
C. Risk exposure **D.** Risk evaluation

Q.36 How many compressions and breaths should you do for each cycle of CPR?

A. 15 compressions, 2 breaths
B. 30 compressions, 5 breaths
C. 30 compressions, 2 breaths
D. 15 compressions, 5 breaths

Q.37 What causes Anaphylactic shock?

A. Choking
B. Insect sting or spider bites
C. 3rd degree burns
D. Heart attack

Q.38 Which is the tank on the back of a toilet?

A. Soap tank **B.** Septic tank
C. Flush tank **D.** None

Q.39 What is the most common kind of litter, by number, found in waterways?

A. Plastic bags **B.** Plastic bottles
C. Aluminium cans **D.** All of the above

Q.40 The radiant efficiency of the luminous source depends on:

A. The shape of the source
B. The temperature of the source
C. The wavelength of the light rays
D. All of the above

Winning and Working

Q.41 Arrange the following coal mines of India from east to west:

1. Bokaro
2. Adilabad
3. Raniganj
4. Bishrampur

Choose the correct option from the codes given below:

A. 3,2,1,4 **B.** 2,1,4,3 **C.** 3,1,4,2 **D.** 2,3,1,4

Q.42 Bishrampur is famous for which of the following mines?

A. Iron ore **B.** Coal
C. Manganese **D.** Copper ore

Q.43 The branch of geology which deals with the morphology, classification, mechanism and causes of development of these rock structures is called as __________

A. rock geology **B.** structural geology
C. basic geology **D.** lithology

Q.44 Stratification can be seen widely in which of the following rocks?

A. Igneous rocks **B.** Metamorphic rocks
C. Sedimentary rocks **D.** Fossil rocks

Q.45 The methods of site investigation are dependent upon _______

A. Climatic condition
B. Nature of the engineering project
C. Local topography
D. All of the above

Q.46 When the material collected to represent a rock type, or a formation of an ore body in the quantitative sense then it is termed as:

A. specimen
B. sample
C. both specimen and sample can be used
D. quantitative specimen

Q.47 For drilling operation, the drill rotates with____ pressure if the job is held on earth.

A. upward
B. downward
C. 45° inclined to both planes
D. none of the mentioned

Q.48 Which of the following operation, we can't perform on drilling machine?

A. Reaming **B.** Tapping
C. Lapping **D.** None of the above

Q.49 Tapping attachment is included in______ method of tool holding devices.

A. by chucks
B. by sleeve
C. by directly fitting in the spindle
D. none of the above

Q.50 Floating holder is included in_____ method of tool holding devices.

A. directly fitting in the spindle
B. special attachments
C. a socket
D. none of the above

Q.51 When a misfire is suspected, no one shall enter the blast area for:

A. 30 minutes if safety fuses and blasting caps are used.
B. 45 minutes if any other type of detonators are used.
C. 20 minutes if safety fuses and blasting caps are used.
D. 55 minutes if any other type of detonators are used.

Q.52 If explosive material is suspected of burning at a blast site, persons must be evacuated from the area and not permitted to return for at least ____ hour(s) after the burning of suspected burning has stopped.

A. 1/2 **B.** 1 **C.** 2 **D.** 4

Q.53 The slope of the stress-strain curve in the elastic deformation region is:

A. Elastic modulus **B.** Plastic modulus
C. Poisson's ratio **D.** None of the above

Q.54 What is the stress-strain curve?

A. It is the percentage of stress and stain.
B. It is the relationship between stress and strain.
C. It is the difference between stress and strain.
D. None of the mentioned.

Q.55 Which point on the stress strain curve occurs after the proportionality limit?

A. Upper yield point **B.** Lower yield point
C. Elastic limit **D.** Ultimate point

Q.56 A rock made up of quartz will have a very similar composition to:

A. igneous rocks **B.** metamorphic rocks
C. sedimentary rocks **D.** quartz

Q.57 An instrument in which the value of the ethnical quantity to be measured can be determined from the deflection of the instrument when it has been precalibrated by comparison with an absolute instrument:

A. absolute instrument
B. secondary instrument
C. recording instrument
D. integrating instrument

Q.58 The P-wave of a seismic event always arrives:

A. before the S-wave
B. at the same time as S-wave
C. after the S–wave
D. none of the above

Q.59 RQD stands for:

A. Rock Quality Deficiency
B. Rock Quality Designation
C. Rock Quantity Designation
D. Rock Quantity Deficiency

Q.60 Which of the following is not a method of control of mass movement?

A. Afforestation
B. Retaining wall
C. Chemical treatment of rocks
D. Deforestation

Surface environment, Mine Ventilation and Hazards

Q.61 EIA is defined as:

A. A process of identifying, predicting, and evaluating the likely impacts of a proposed project or development to define mitigation actions to reduce negative impacts and to provide positive contributions to the natural environment and well-being.

B. A report was written by government representatives on the planned development impacts of the environment, socio-economic issues and culture.

C. Project life-cycle assessment.

D. None of the above.

Q.62 How many countries have legislation on EIA?

A. More than 100 **B.** Less than 100
C. Less than 50 **D.** None of the above

Q.63 A core part of Impact Management is developing an EMP – environmental management plan. Please indicate which items from the list below are the contents of the EMP.

1. Mitigation
2. Monitoring
3. Capacity Development
4. Implementation Schedule and Cost Estimates
5. Contingency plans
6. TOR

A. 2,3,4 **B.** 1,2,3,4,5
C. 1,2,3,4,5,6 **D.** None of the above

Q.64 Impact Management plans are often____

A. non-compulsory
B. compulsory
C. some time compulsory
D. never compulsory

Q.65 In areas where light rains are uniformly distributed throughout the year, the type of sewerage system to be adopted is:

A. separate system
B. combined system
C. partially combined system
D. none of the above

Q.66 The pH value of sewage is determined with the help of:

A. imhoff cone **B.** turbidimeter
C. potentiometer **D.** none of the above

Q.67 Where is Methane most likely to be found in a mine?

A. Near to **B.** Away from the roof
C. In the pipeline **D.** Near the body

Q.68 What are the sources of Hydrogen in a mine?

A. Charging batteries **B.** Mine fires
C. Explosions **D.** All of the above

Q.69 When is the oxygen (O_2) level in air considered to be dangerous:

A. when the oxygen (O_2) level falls below 36%.
B. when the oxygen (O_2) level falls below 76%.
C. when the oxygen (O_2) level falls below 16%.
D. when the oxygen (O_2) level falls below 6%.

Q.70 What is the percentage of oxygen in intake air into mines?

A. 20.28 % **B.** 78.04 % **C.** 21 % **D.** 25 %

Q.71 What percent of carbon monoxide can cause death in less than one hour?

A. 0.2 percent or less **B.** 1.6 percent or more
C. 0.15 percent **D.** 0.1 percent or less

Q.72 Why is it important to prefer ash handling systems?

A. Coal ash produced destroys the machinery by entering into them
B. Coal ash produced annually accounts for thousands of tones
C. Coal ash can be reutilized for some other purpose
D. Coal ash affects the health of people working at plants

Q.73 The decay of timber by fungus growth is caused by:

A. CH_4 **B.** O_2 absorption
C. N_2 depletion **D.** CO_2

Q.74 Each 1 % reduction in the O_2 % results in about the depletion from the Safety light is:

A. 10 %. **B.** 20 %. **C.** 30 %. **D.** 40 %.

Q.75 The light of the safety lamp is extinguished when O_2 % falls to?

A. 19 % **B.** 17.5 % **C.** 21 % **D.** 20 %

Q.76 Mining laws in India require that mine air should contain a minimum % of O_2 is?

A. 25 % **B.** 21 % **C.** 19 % **D.** 17 %

Q.77 ____________ is/are especially useful for rescue teams to use when they need to flush out or ventilate a small area of the mine.

A. Bulkheads **B.** Line brattice
C. Stoppings **D.** A and C

Q.78 Air locks are used by mine rescue teams ____________

A. to establish a fresh air base.
B. when opening a door or knocking out a bulkhead behind which conditions are not definitely known.
C. before opening a barricade in bad air behind which trapped miners may be located.
D. all of the above

Q.79 To detect oxygen ________ atmospheres teams will use an ________ indicator.

A. poor, hydrogen **B.** enriched, methane
C. deficient, oxygen **D.** none of the above

Q.80 In some mines, carbon dioxide is liberated from the ______________.

A. rock strata **B.** mine roof
C. mine floor **D.** none of the above

Mine Machineries, surveying and electricity

Q.81 ___________ is a self propelled machine which is used mainly to exert a powerful tractive force for pulling other machines.

A. Tractor **B.** Bulldozer
C. Angle dozer **D.** Scraper

Q.82 A _________ is used to level the ground and spreads the loose material.

A. excavator **B.** scraper
C. grader **D.** tractor

Q.83 Material handling consists of movement of material from:

A. one machine to another
B. one shop to another shop
C. stores to shop
D. all of the above

Q.84 Economy in material handling can be achieved by:

A. employing gravity feed movements.
B. minimizing the distance of travel.
C. by carrying material to destination without using manual labour.
D. all of the above.

Q.85 The Principle of 'Unit load' states that:

A. Materials should be moved in lots.
B. One unit should be moved at a time.
C. Both (A) and (B)
D. None of the above

Q.86 According to Herzberg, which of the following is a maintenance factor?

A. Salary **B.** Work itself
C. Responsibility **D.** Recognition

Q.87 Type of surveying in which the mean surface of the earth is considered as a plane and the spheroidal shape is neglected called as ______.

A. topographic surveying
B. hydrographic surveying
C. geodetic surveying
D. plane surveying

Q.88 Type of surveying in which the shape of the earth taking into account is ________.

A. topographic surveying
B. hydrographic surveying
C. geodetic surveying
D. plane surveying

Q.89 The Horizontal projection of an area and shows only horizontal distances of the points is ________.

A. contour lines **B.** levelling
C. surveying **D.** plan

Q.90 Determining the absolute location of any point or the absolute location and direction of any line on the surface of the earth is called ______.

A. topographic surveying
B. astronomical surveying
C. cadastral surveying
D. hydrographic surveying

Q.91 Subdivision/layout plan which shall be drawn on a scale of not less than:

A. 1:100 **B.** 1:500 **C.** 1:1000 **D.** 1:50

Q.92 The plan of the buildings and elevations and sections accompanying the notice shall be drawn to a scale ________.

A. 1:10 **B.** 1:50 **C.** 1:100 **D.** 1:500

Q.93 A _________ usually parallels to the plot boundaries and laid down in each case by the Authority, beyond which nothing can be constructed towards the site boundaries.

A. building line **B.** control line
C. property line **D.** plot line

Q.94 The ratio of the total floor area inclusive of all the floors to the area of the plot on which the building stands is known as _________.

A. groundage **B.** plot area
C. floor area **D.** built-up area

Q.95 What is the prominent point on the chain line and can be either at the beginning of the chain line or at the end?

A. Subsidiary station **B.** Surveyor station
C. Main station **D.** Tie stations

Q.96 The book in which the chain or tape measurements are entered is called the ______

A. assistant book **B.** surveyor book
C. field book **D.** survey book

Q.97 The chain line may be represented either by a single line or by two lines spaced about ___ to ____ cm apart.

A. 1.5 to 2 **B.** 2 to 3
C. 1.5 to 2.5 **D.** 2.5 to 3.5

Q.98 Which of the following details need not be given at the beginning of a particular chain survey?

A. Date of survey
B. Names of surveyors
C. Details of survey lines
D. Type of soil

Q.99 Which of the following can be affected by atmospheric path disturbances?

A. Modern GPS surveying
B. Conventional GPS
C. Absolute positioning
D. Resection method

Q.100 Which among the following can be described as an application of pseudo ranging?

A. Computation of distance between satellite and user

B. Computation of distance between GPS antenna and satellite

C. Computation of distance between GPS antenna and user

D. Computation of distance between satellite and object

// Smart Answer Sheet //

Correct — Percentage of students who answered correctly. Skipped — Percentage of students who skipped.

Q.	Ans.	Correct / Skipped	Q.	Ans.	Correct / Skipped	Q.	Ans.	Correct / Skipped	Q.	Ans.	Correct / Skipped	Q.	Ans.	Correct / Skipped	Q.	Ans.	Correct / Skipped
1	A	63.23 % / 1.69 %	18	B	84.83 % / 0.0 %	35	C	84.48 % / 0.0 %	52	B	78.86 % / 0.0 %	69	C	17.68 % / 3.65 %	86	A	77.33 % / 0.0 %
2	C	81.12 % / 0.0 %	19	D	51.9 % / 1.23 %	36	C	78.59 % / 0.0 %	53	A	56.51 % / 1.14 %	70	C	42.89 % / 1.09 %	87	D	60.76 % / 1.72 %
3	D	63.75 % / 1.62 %	20	B	68.14 % / 1.65 %	37	B	17.83 % / 3.49 %	54	B	76.81 % / 0.0 %	71	B	13.57 % / 4.82 %	88	C	45.09 % / 1.03 %
4	D	87.36 % / 0.0 %	21	D	78.95 % / 0.0 %	38	C	40.27 % / 1.68 %	55	C	14.78 % / 4.22 %	72	B	19.85 % / 4.02 %	89	D	83.99 % / 0.0 %
5	A	55.82 % / 1.76 %	22	D	40.49 % / 1.92 %	39	D	64.04 % / 1.73 %	56	D	78.98 % / 0.0 %	73	B	69.88 % / 1.08 %	90	B	54.51 % / 1.19 %
6	A	89.74 % / 0.0 %	23	B	51.21 % / 1.43 %	40	B	44.12 % / 1.76 %	57	B	31.13 % / 4.52 %	74	C	10.75 % / 3.27 %	91	B	21.99 % / 3.68 %
7	A	85.1 % / 0.0 %	24	A	68.91 % / 1.93 %	41	C	69.58 % / 1.18 %	58	A	43.84 % / 1.59 %	75	B	40.81 % / 1.19 %	92	C	51.44 % / 1.3 %
8	A	46.31 % / 1.13 %	25	A	62.45 % / 1.83 %	42	B	87.75 % / 0.0 %	59	B	66.83 % / 1.32 %	76	C	53.35 % / 1.22 %	93	A	68.52 % / 1.07 %
9	B	21.12 % / 3.95 %	26	B	63.48 % / 1.98 %	43	B	52.66 % / 1.42 %	60	D	45.15 % / 1.6 %	77	B	54.15 % / 1.99 %	94	D	85.39 % / 0.0 %
10	C	59.41 % / 1.15 %	27	B	89.22 % / 0.0 %	44	C	44.68 % / 1.93 %	61	A	22.45 % / 4.16 %	78	D	65.78 % / 1.53 %	95	C	27.18 % / 4.61 %
11	C	44.77 % / 1.65 %	28	A	65.93 % / 1.65 %	45	B	77.27 % / 0.0 %	62	A	77.28 % / 0.0 %	79	C	63.2 % / 1.89 %	96	C	77.83 % / 0.0 %
12	B	83.48 % / 0.0 %	29	C	47.47 % / 1.13 %	46	B	16.84 % / 3.35 %	63	B	20.05 % / 4.92 %	80	B	49.08 % / 1.99 %	97	A	58.3 % / 1.68 %
13	B	54.8 % / 1.3 %	30	A	47.96 % / 1.84 %	47	B	52.81 % / 1.08 %	64	B	88.2 % / 0.0 %	81	A	17.12 % / 3.47 %	98	D	53.39 % / 1.31 %
14	A	89.14 % / 0.0 %	31	B	67.3 % / 1.72 %	48	D	42.82 % / 1.01 %	65	B	76.26 % / 0.0 %	82	C	66.37 % / 1.05 %	99	A	62.76 % / 1.07 %
15	D	58.9 % / 1.63 %	32	D	89.76 % / 0.0 %	49	D	55.51 % / 1.55 %	66	C	46.36 % / 1.88 %	83	D	45.88 % / 1.81 %	100	B	66.98 % / 1.6 %
16	D	61.83 % / 1.12 %	33	A	51.28 % / 1.05 %	50	B	19.79 % / 4.69 %	67	A	46.99 % / 1.11 %	84	D	18.05 % / 4.51 %			
17	C	60.69 % / 1.42 %	34	D	47.58 % / 1.78 %	51	A	61.88 % / 1.06 %	68	D	67.47 % / 1.97 %	85	A	64.87 % / 1.78 %			

//Hints and Solutions//

1. India win the 2022 U19 World Cup title, by beating England by 4 wickets Shaik Rasheed and Nishant Sindhu cracked the 50 s in chase of 190 as India clinched record-extending fifth U19 World Cup title in Antigua.

Raj Bawa claimed a fifer while Ravi Kumar bagged 4 wickets to fold England for 189 BCCI president Sourav Ganguly announced a cash prize of 40 lakhs.

Hence, the correct option is (A).

2. Raja Todar Mal was the Finance Minister of the Mughal empire during Akbar's reign. He was one of the Navaratnas in Akbar's durbar. As a finance minister of Akbar, he introduced a new system of revenue known as 'Zabt' and a system of taxation called 'Dahshala'.

Hence, the correct option is (C).

3. The Paithan (Jayakwadi) Hydro-electric project, completed with the help of Japan, is on the Godavari river.

Jayakwadi dam is an earthen dam located on the Godavari river at the site of Jayakwadi village in Paithan taluka of Aurangabad district in Maharashtra, India.

Jayakwadi is one of the largest earthen dams in Asia. It is height is approx 41.30 m and length of 9.998 km (10 km approx) with a total storage capacity of 2,909 MCM (million cubic meters) and an effective live storage capacity is 2,171 MCM. The total catchment area of the dam is 21,750 km^2. There are total 27 gates of for the dam. Jayakwadi Dam is also called Nathsagar Dam.

Hence, the correct option is (D).

4. Actress Shruti Haasan has been roped in to play the character of Elsa in Disney's sequel to the global blockbuster animated film from 2013, Frozen. Shruti will also be singing three songs in the Tamil dubbed version of Frozen 2. The Hindi dubbed version of Frozen 2 will feature the voices of Priyanka Chopra Jonas and Parineeti Chopra while the Telugu dubbed version will feature Nithya Menen.

Hence, the correct option is (D).

5. "MyLab", a molecular diagnostic company based at Pune, became the first company in India to get Covid 19 test kits validated by the Drug Controller of India. The validation of the Reverse transcription-polymerase chain reaction (RT-PCR) tests kits developed by the company has been validated by the National Institute of Virology.

Hence, the correct option is (A).

6. The 'Anti-leprosy day' is observed annually on the last Sunday of January, across the world. This year, the day is observed on January 26, 2020, the month's last Sunday.

The World Health Organisation has adopted a theme of 'Leprosy isn't you think' to create awareness to fight the prejudice and discrimination associated with the disease. In India, the Confederation of Indian Industry (CII) signed an MoU with the charitable organization- Sasakawa India Leprosy Foundation (S-ILF) to eradicate leprosy in the country.

Hence, the correct option is (A).

7. The Preamble to the Indian Constitution is based on the 'Objectives Resolution', drafted and moved by Pandit Jawaharlal Nehru before the Drafting Committee of the Constitution and adopted by the Constituent Assembly. It has been amended by the 42nd Constitutional Amendment Act (1976), which added three new words—socialist, secular and integrity.

Hence, the correct option is (A).

8. A no-confidence motion against the Union Government can be initiated only in the Lok Sabha (the lower house of the Parliament of India). Council of Ministers is collectively responsible to Lok Sabha and it remains in office till it enjoys the confidence of the majority of the members in Lok Sabha. Thus, a motion of no-confidence is moved to remove the council of ministers and thus oust the government from office.

Following are conditions of No-confidence motion:

- No-confidence motion can be moved only in Lok Sabha. It is not allowed in Rajya Sabha.
- It is moved against the entire Council of Ministers and not individual ministers or private members.
- The motion is admitted for discussion when a minimum of 50 members of the house support the motion (under rule 198 of Lok Sabha Rules 16th edition).

Hence, the correct option is (A).

9. Louis Pasteur discovered that some molecules have mirror images of each other and explained them as left-handed and right-handed versions of a chemical compound. In 1848, Louis Pasteur discovered that the para tartrate (A chemical molecule) actually consists of two different kinds of crystals that can be clearly discerned under a microscope. Using tweezers, he separated the crystals and dissolved them in separate solutions. Passing polarized light through each of the solutions, he found that one solution twisted the light to the right and the other an equal angle to the left. The reason the unseparated para tartrate solution had no effect on the polarized light beam, Pasteur realized, was that the light-twisting effects of its two enantiomers canceled each other out. The reason the constituents behave oppositely is that their molecules are mirror images of each other.

Hence, the correct option is (B).

10. The GST Council has decided on a four-tier tax structure of 5%, 12%, 18% and 28% to cover most goods and services. Apart from this, a cess will be levied on demerit and luxury goods on top of the peak rate. This cess will be used to create a fund and this fund will be used to compensate the states which face the loss of revenue due to GST implementation.

Hence, the correct option is (C).

11. Descriptions of customer satisfaction with products and services are examples of external information in an organization. Customer satisfaction is defined as a measurement that determines how happy customers are with a company's products, services and capabilities. Customer satisfaction information, including surveys and ratings, can help a company determine how to best improve or changes its products and services.

Hence, the correct option is (C).

12. The purpose of job enrichment is to increase job efficiency. Job enrichment refers to the structuring of jobs to involve higher-level conceptual thinking and responsibility so that employees can make decisions that were formerly the prerogative of superior managers. According to Keith Davis, "Job enrichment means additional motivators added to the job so that it (job) is more rewarding, although the term has come to be applied to any effort to humanize jobs".

We can say that job enrichment encourages growth and self-actualization. It increases motivation and improves performance and thus provides more productive and more lively jobs.

Hence, the correct option is (B).

13. Strategic planning as a broad concept consists of **strategy formulation and strategy implementation**. The concept of strategic planning originally became popular in the 1950s and 1960s. Strategic planning is the art of creating specific business strategies, implementing them, and evaluating the results of executing the plan, in regard to a company's overall long-term goals or desires. It is a concept that focuses on integrating various departments (such as accounting and finance, marketing, and human resources) within a company to accomplish its strategic goals. The term strategic planning is essentially synonymous with strategic management.

Hence, the correct option is (B).

14. Organization structure primarily refers to how activities are coordinated & controlled.

An organizational structure defines the manner in which the roles, power, authority, and responsibilities are assigned and governed, and depicts how information flows between the different levels of hierarchy in an organization.

Hence, the correct option is (A).

15. Distinctiveness refers to how unique the behavior is to a particular situation. There is a low distinctiveness if an individual behaves similarly in all situations, and there exists a high distinctiveness when the person only shows the behavior in particular situations.

Hence, the correct option is (D).

16. The critical path method (CPM) is a project modeling technique that is used by project managers to find important deadlines and deliver a project on time. In a project, the critical path is the longest distance between the start and the finish, including all the tasks and their duration. Once a critical path is determined, you'll have a clear picture of the project's actual schedule.

Hence, the correct option is (D).

17. Break-Even Analysis in economics, business, and cost accounting refers to the point in which total cost and total revenue are equal. The break-even point (BEP) or break-even level represents the sales amount—in either unit (quantity) or revenue (sales) terms—that is required to cover total costs, consisting of both fixed and variable costs to the company. Total profit at the break-even point is zero.

Total cost = Fixed cost + Variable cost.

Hence, the correct option is (C).

18. An investment is an asset or item acquired with the goal of generating income or appreciation. Appreciation refers to an increase in the value of an asset over time. When an individual purchases a good as an investment, the intent is not to consume the good but rather to use it in the future to create wealth. An investment always concerns the outlay of some asset today—time, money, or effort—in hopes of a greater payoff in the future than what was originally put in.

Hence, the correct option is (B).

19. The Occupational Safety and Health Act (OSH Act) was enacted by Congress in 1970 and authorized the Secretary of Labour to establish Federal standards to ensure safe workplace conditions.

To assure safe and healthful working conditions for working men and women; by authorizing enforcement of the standards developed under the Act; by assisting and encouraging the States in their efforts to assure safe and healthful working conditions; by providing for research, information, education, and training in the field of occupational safety and health; and for other purposes.

Hence, the correct option is (D).

20. Purchasing responsibilities can be divided into Buying Clerical and Traffic division.

The person that generally runs the purchasing department is called the Purchasing Manager – sometimes in larger companies, they may be deemed an executive e.g. Director, VP, or Chief Procurement Officer (CPO). The purchasing or procurement manager runs the purchasing department These highly trained professionals are responsible for crafting effective procurement strategies, finding cost-effective deals and suppliers, and suppliers, and supply chain management from initial requisition to invoice to invoice payment. They evaluate and bury raw materials. products, and services while creating strategies to cut costs and meet company objectives.

Hence, the correct option is (B).

21. Coal mine disasters in West Bengal are due to flooding.

Flooding cause mines to get high pressurized, due to which there is less time for vacating the mine.

Hence, the correct option is (D).

22. Program Evaluation and Review Technique (PERT) is a method used to examine the tasks that are in a schedule and determine a variation of the Critical Path Method (CPM). It analyses the time to complete each task and it is associated dependencies to determine the minimum time to complete a project.

There are three estimation times involved in PERT; Optimistic Time Estimate (TOPT), Most Likely Time Estimate (TLIKELY), and Pessimistic Time Estimate (TPESS). In PERT, these three estimate times are derived for each activity.

Hence, the correct option is (D).

23. Periodical medical examination is carried out every 5 years.

A Periodic Medical Examination (PME) focuses on any (occupational) health damage risks concerning employees within your company. The examination looks at the lifestyle, workability and health of your employees.

Hence, the correct option is (B).

24. The remuneration for the members of the committee shall be fixed by the Central Govt.

The Remuneration/compensation/commission etc. to be paid to Managing Director/Whole-time Director/Key Managerial Personnel shall be governed as per provisions of the Companies Act, 2013 and rules made thereunder or any other enactment for the time being in force or as per the policy of the Company & ongoing industrial norms.

Hence, the correct option is (A).

25. The workmen inspector shall be employed if the number of persons employed exceeds 500 workers in a mine.

Employee's inspectors are elected by a majority of persons employed at mines in a designated mining district and are appointed to the position by the State Mining Engineer. Employee's inspectors provide an additional avenue for mine workers to consult about safety and health.

Hence, the correct option is (A).

26. Small hydrogen explosions, known as hydrogen "pops" are fairly common in firefighting. The bigger hazard with hydrogen is the possibility of it accumulating to a large enough extent to cause a violent explosion.

Hence, the correct option is (B).

27. High voltage is defined as a voltage higher than 1,000 volts.

The definition is based on safety considerations or the voltage where arcing will occur. There is no universally accepted definition. The International Electrotechnical Commission and its national counterparts (IET, IEEE, VDE, etc.) define high voltage as above 1000 V for alternating current, and at least 1500 V for direct current.

Hence, the correct option is (B).

28. A Runaway switch is used in connection with direct rope haulage.

Run Away Switch: This switch is normally kept open by a spring. When a lever handle is operated by an operator, the switch gets closed. And tubs can pass over it otherwise the tub derails when they pass over the runaway switch. It is used with direct rope haulage & main & tail rope haulage.

Hence, the correct option is (A).

29. Further, Section 11A of the Maternity Act safeguards the intent of Section 48 of the Factories Act, 1948, which requires factories with more than 30 female workers to have a creche.

The Maternity Benefit (Amendment) Act, 2017(hereinafter referred to as the "Maternity Act") is a landmark law that has enhanced the maternity benefits already available under the parent Maternity Benefit Act,1961. The Act has increased the duration of paid maternity leave available to working mothers from 12 weeks to 26 weeks. However, women, who already have two surviving children will be only entitled to a paid maternity leave of 12 weeks.

Hence, the correct option is (C).

30. Side Discharge Loader is a Crawler mounted machine.

A crawler excavator (or crawling digger) is a tracked vehicle designed to dig or grade, or move earth and large objects, and is classified by its mode of locomotion. The many types of excavators include wheeled, walker, towed and rail excavators.

Hence, the correct option is (A).

31. The minimum wages act comes in 1948.

Minimum wages have been defined as "the minimum amount of remuneration that an employer is required to pay wage earners for the work performed during a given period, which cannot be reduced by collective agreement or an individual contract".

The purpose of minimum wages is to protect workers against unduly low pay. They help ensure a just and equitable share of the fruits of progress to all, and a minimum living wage to all who are employed and in need of such protection. Minimum wages can also be one element of a policy to overcome poverty and reduce inequality, including those between men and women, by promoting the right to equal remuneration for work of equal value.

Hence, the correct option is (B).

32. The responsibility for the maintenance of employee health and safety is with employees, employers and the government.

Maintenance workers, also known as repair workers, fix and maintain mechanical equipment, buildings, and machines. Tasks include plumbing work, painting, flooring repair and upkeep, electrical repairs and heating and air conditioning system maintenance.

Hence, the correct option is (D).

33. Ensuring the safety, health and welfare of the employees is the primary purpose of the Factories Act, 1948.

The main objective of the Act is not only to ensure adequate safety measures but also to promote the health and welfare of the workers employed in factories as well as to prevent haphazard growth of factories.

Hence, the correct option is (A).

34. Risk management is the responsibility of a whole project team. They should identify the risks as early as possible and come up with ways to deal with them.

Hence, the correct option is (D).

35. The RE represents the risk exposure and it is also called risk impact. RE is defined by the probability of the risk and the loss. Also, a relation of RE is given as:

Risk Exposure = Probability $\times$ Impact.

In an organization risk exposure is the statistically measurable value where impact and probability are assigned on a scale of $1-5$ or $1-10$. Risk Exposure is also called a Risk Priority Number(RPN).

Hence, the correct option is (C).

36. CPR – or Cardiopulmonary Resuscitation – is an emergency lifesaving procedure performed when the heart stops beating.

It is a cycle of 30 chest compressions and 2 rescue breaths. It is given until the patient begins to recover or emergency help arrives.

Hence, the correct option is (C).

37. The terms "anaphylaxis" and "anaphylactic shock" are often used to mean the same thing. They both refer to a severe allergic reaction.

It can occur within seconds or minutes of exposure to something you're allergic to, such as peanuts, bee stings or spider bites.

Hence, the correct option is (B).

38. The back part of the toilet that holds the water used for flushing is called Flush tank. When the tank is empty, the float ball falls freely allowing the valve to open, filling the tank. The refill and overflow tube work together to help keep water in the tank. The overflow tube empties directly into the toilet bowl below, refilling the bowl after a flush.

Hence, the correct option is (C).

39. Fast-food wrappers, bottles, cans, and cigarette butts are more than 80% of the litter we find in our waterways. In the United State, they have 4.6% of the world's population but produce about 33% of the world's solid waste.

Hence, the correct option is (D).

40. When an electric current is passed through a conductor, some heat is produced to I^2R loss, which increases its temperature of the conductor. At low temperatures, the conductor radiates energy in the form of heatwaves, but at very high temperatures, radiated energy will be in the form of light as well as heatwaves.

Radiant efficiency is defined as the ratio of energy radiated in the form of light, produces the sensation of vision to the total energy radiated out by the luminous body'.

Radiant Efficiency = Energy Radiated in the form of light/total energy radiated by the body.s. It is found that maximum radiant efficiency would occur at about 62000° C and even then the value of this maximum efficiency would be 20%.

Hence, the correct option is (B).

41. Correct order will be as 3 -Raniganj (West Bengal), 1-Bokaro (Jharkhand), 4-Bishrampur (Chattisgarh), 2-Adilabad (Northern Telangana).

Hence, the correct option is (C).

42. The Bisrampur is a large coal field located in the east of India in Chhattisgarh. Bisrampur represents one of the largest coal reserves in India having estimated reserves of 1.61 billion tonnes of coal.

Hence, the correct option is (B).

43. The basic definition of structural geology is "the branch of geology which deals with the morphology, classification, mechanism, and causes of the development of these rock structures". The primary goal of structural geology is to use measurements of present-day rock geometries to uncover information about the history of deformation (strain) in the rocks, and ultimately, to understand the stress field that resulted in the observed strain and geometries.

Hence, the correct option is (B).

44. Stratification can be seen widely in the Sedimentary rocks.

Most sedimentary rocks are deposited under conditions that favor the development of distinct layers piled up one above another, from bottom to top. These layers also called beds or strata.

Hence, the correct option is (C).

45. The methods of site investigation are dependent upon the nature of the engineering project.

Site Investigation is the process of collecting information, assessment of the data, and reporting potential hazards beneath a site that is unknown. Site Investigation is grouped into the following stages: Soil Investigation. Geologic survey maps Preliminary investigation.

Hence, the correct option is (B).

46. Sampling is defined as taking a small portion of a whole mass that accurately represents the whole mass. Since this site is primarily concerned with mining and mining issues, the sampling discussed here will be relative to mining, sampling of ores and processed products from mills, processing plants and mines.

Hence, the correct option is (B).

47. For drilling operation, the drill rotates with downward pressure if the job is held on earth. Drilling is a cutting process that uses a drill bit to cut a hole of circular cross-section in solid materials. The drill bit is usually a rotary cutting tool, often multi-point. The bit is pressed against the work-piece and rotated at rates from hundreds to thousands of revolutions per minute.

Hence, the correct option is (B).

48. Although drilling is primarily intended for drill now it becomes a versatile tool. It can perform various operations including reaming, tapping, lapping and so on.

Hence, the correct option is (D).

49. It is included in the special attachment method. In tapping, one end is always thinner than another end.

Hence, the correct option is (D).

50. A Floating holder has included in the special attachment of tool holding devices. A Floating holder is a type of holder that permits a certain amount of freedom to enable the tool with the purpose of maintaining a proper path relative to the work.

Hence, the correct option is (B).

51. When a misfire is suspected, no one shall enter the blast area for 30 minutes if safety fuses and blasting caps are used.

Misfire means the complete or partial failure of a blasting charge to explode as planned. In any of these circumstances, there may be a risk of danger to the operator or to the public, particularly from fly-rock in the event of a detonation. Unexploded charges may need to be recovered by hand.

Hence, the correct option is (A).

52. If an explosive material is suspected of burning at a blast site, persons must be evacuated from the area and not permitted to return for at least 1 hour(s) after the burning of suspected burning has stopped.

Mining explosives are substances that detonate to produce a high-intensity shock wave and large volumes of gas which, being confined in a hole, expand rapidly, entering existing minor cracks in the rock, and creating new cracks to break the rock.

Hence, the correct option is (B).

53. The slope of the stress-strain curve in the elastic deformation region is the modulus of elasticity, which is known as Young's modulus. It represents the stiffness of the material-resistance to elastic strain. The description of Hooke's law can also be found from the slope. According to Hook's law, the elastic modulus is the ratio of stress and strain.

Hence, the correct option is (A).

54. The relationship between stress and strain on a graph is the stress-strain curve. It represents the change in stress with the change in strain. It is obtained by gradually applying a load to a test sample and measuring the deformation, from which the stress and strain can be determined.

Hence, the correct option is (B).

55. The curve will be stress-strain proportional up to the proportionality limit. After these, the elastic limit will occur.

A material's elastic limit is the greatest stress that can be applied to it without causing plastic (permanent) deformation. When a material is stressed to a point below its elastic limit, it will return to its original length once the stress is removed.

Hence, the correct option is (C).

56. Quartz is a defining constituent of granite and other felsic igneous rocks. It is very common in sedimentary rocks such as sandstone and shale. It is a common constituent of schist, gneiss, quartzite and other metamorphic rocks.

Hence, the correct option is (D).

57. Secondary instruments are so constructed that the value of current, voltage or other quantity to be measured can be determined from the malefaction of the instruments, only if the latter has been calibrated by comparison with either an absolute instrument or one which has already been calibrated. The deflection obtained is meaningless until such calibration has been made.

Hence, the correct option is (B).

58. The P-wave of a seismic event always arrives before. P waves travel the fastest and are the first to arrive from the earthquake. In S or shear waves, rock oscillates perpendicular to the direction of wave propagation. In rock. S waves generally travel about 60% the speed of waves, and the S wave always arrives after the P wave.

Hence, the correct option is (A).

59. RQD stands for Rock Quality Designation. The Rock-quality designation RQD is a rough measure of the degree of jointing or fracture in a rock mass, measured as a percentage of the drill core in lengths of 10 cm or more. High-quality rock has an RQD of more than 75%, low quality of less than 50%.

Hence, the correct option is (B).

60. The widely adopted methods for control of mass movements include the construction of retaining walls, chemical treatment of rocks, rock bolting and to some extent, afforestation can avoid mass movements, but, deforestation promotes mass movements.

Hence, the correct option is (D).

61. Environmental impact assessment (EIA) is an environmental decision support tool, which provides information on the likely impacts of development projects to those who take the decision as to whether the project should be authorized. The purpose of an EIA is to determine the potential environmental, social, and health effects of a proposed development so that those who take the decisions in developing the project and in authorizing the project are informed about the likely consequences of their decisions before they take those decisions and are thereby more accountable. It is intended to facilitate informed and transparent decision-making while seeking to avoid, reduce, or mitigate potential adverse impacts through the consideration of alternative options, sites, or processes.

Hence, the correct option is (A).

62. EIA has been implemented through a diverse range of legal mechanisms around the world. It is currently practiced in more than "100" countries. The first comprehensive legislation for EIA came into force on 1 January 1970 in the United States of America by the National Environmental Policy Act (NEPA) 1969. The USA sought to reverse what was a 'clear and intensifying trend towards environmental degradation' (Holland 1985). In brief, there are three main elements to the legislation:

- A general policy for the environment.
- The requirement for the preparation of an EIS for 'major federal actions significantly affecting the quality of the human environment'.
- The establishment of the Council on Environmental Quality (CEQ) to administer the legislation and to uphold the quality of EISs.

Hence, the correct option is (A).

63. The TOR is not part of the EMP. TORs give guidelines for the EIA report content and they are created during the scoping phase.

A core part of impact management is developing an **Environmental Management Plan (EMP),** which forms the basis for impact management during project construction and operation, and outlines activities for continuous monitoring. It also translates recommended mitigation measures into specific actions that will be carried out by the project proponent. The typical elements of EMPs can be summarized as follows:

- Mitigation measures: Summary of all mitigation measures and details on how these will be implemented; the measures are linked to the impact analyses.
- Monitoring: The plans for monitoring the environmental impacts and the effectiveness of mitigation measures in addressing the impacts.
- Capacity Development: The assessment of capacity-building needs required to involve stakeholders in managing environmental and social impacts and monitoring efforts.
- Implementation Schedule and Cost Estimates: Costs of the outlined mitigation activities, capacity-building and monitoring; this will include the cost of implementation and then ongoing monitoring and follow-up capacity development costs.
- Integration of the EMP with the project: The EMP needs to be developed in a way that fits with the planned project, the mitigation actions, and other activities linked to the project.
- **Contingency plan:** The EIA must include an assessment of possible risks and external contingencies (natural events and disasters) relevant to the proposed project activities, identifying and determining those that pose risks or threats to the health of the population and the structure of ecosystems.

Hence, the correct option is (B).

64. Impact Management plans are often compulsory.

The Environmental Management Plan (EMP) is the plan constructed during the process of EIA that provides a description of the methods and procedures for mitigating and monitoring impacts EMP's outline the environmental impacts, the mitigation measures, roles and responsibilities, timescales and cost of mitigation.

Hence, the correct option is (B).

65. In areas where light rains are uniformly distributed throughout the year, the type of sewerage system to be adopted is a combined system.

A combined sewer is a sewage collection system of pipes and tunnels designed to simultaneously collect surface runoff and sewage water in a shared system.

Hence, the correct option is (B).

66. The pH value of sewage is determined with the help of a potentiometer.

The potentiometric pH sensor measures the difference in electromotive force (EMF) between a pH sensing electrode and a reference electrode. As a reference electrode, an Ag/AgCl is the most commonly used because of its potential stability and environment friendly.

Hence, the correct option is (C).

67. Methane is lighter than air hence it goes near to the roof. Methane may be found anywhere, but is most likely to be encountered in virgin coal, roof cavities, high places, abandoned workings, and places that are improperly ventilated.

Hence, the correct option is (A).

68. Hydrogen gas (H_2) is another key component in determining if a fire exists. Hydrogen gas is most often generated as a by-product of battery charging. It has been found in limited instances as strata gas. Hydrogen can also be liberated in elevated coal oxidation situations. It is detected at temperatures just below, and in high levels following combustion. Hydrogen can also be created by an interaction between burning coal and water (so-called water gas reaction), at times in very high concentrations (approaching 15%), and can actually exceed carbon monoxide levels. Because of its low (0.070) density relative to the air, if adequate mixing is not taking place, H_2 will most likely be found at the roof. Hydrogen is highly explosive. It is flammable in concentrations from 4% to 74% in air. Low H_2 levels begin to be detected at temperatures just below those required for active coal flaming.

Hence, the correct option is (D).

69. When oxygen level falls below 16%(12 to 16%) considered to be dangerous which causes tachypnea (increased breathing rates), tachycardia (accelerated heartbeat), and impaired attention, thinking, and coordination, even in people who are resting.

Hence, the correct option is (C).

70. The percentage of oxygen in intake air into mine is 21% by volume, N_2 78% by volume and small amounts of other gases including argon, carbon dioxide, neon, helium, and hydrogen. The gas exhaled is 4% to 5% by volume of carbon dioxide.

Hence, the correct option is (C).

71. When the concentration of carbon monoxide becomes equal or more than 1.6 percent (1600 PPM), causes headache, dizziness and nausea within 20 minutes or death within one hour.

When too much carbon monoxide is in the air, the body replaces the oxygen in red blood cells with carbon monoxide. This can lead to serious tissue damage or even death.

Hence, the correct option is (B).

72. Considering the large coal-burning capacity plant of modern times, the amount of ash produced when the coal is burnt is in thousands of tones. It could have an effect on other subjects too if the proper ash handling methods are not followed. And for different environmental, economic and product benefits the coal ash is reused by different types of industries in different ways of its necessity.

Hence, the correct option is (A).

73. The decay of timber by fungus growth is caused by O_2 absorption. Timber decay (rot) is caused by a biological attack within the wood by certain species of fungi. The fungus can lie dormant in the timber for years until the right conditions present themselves. The conditions needed are oxygen, moisture and nutrients, with moisture being the critical component.

Hence, the correct option is (B).

74. Each 1% reduction in the O_2% results in about the depletion from the Safety light is 30%. A safety lamp is any of several types of lamp that provides illumination in coal mines and is designed to operate in air that may contain coal dust or gases, both of which are potentially flammable or explosive.

The methane-air flame is extinguished at about 17% oxygen content (which will still support life).

Hence, the correct option is (C).

75. If the mine air is oxygen-poor (asphyxiant gas), the lamp flame would be extinguished (blackdamp or chokedamp). A light of safety lamp is extinguished at about 17.5% oxygen content (which will still support life), so the lamp gave an early indication of an unhealthy atmosphere, allowing the miners to get out before they died of asphyxiation.

Hence, the correct option is (B).

76. At every place in the mine where persons are required to work or pass, the air does not contain less than 19 percent of oxygen or more than 0.5 percent of carbon dioxide or any noxious gas in quantity likely to affect the health of any person. Hence, mining laws in India require that mine air should contain a minimum "19%" of oxygen.

Hence, the correct option is (C).

77. Line brattice is especially useful for rescue teams to use when they need to flush out or ventilate a small area of the mine.

The Line brattice ventilation system in underground coal mines is used to control the quantity, movement, and direction of air inside the development headings. The quality of the ventilation i.e. the quantity of air and the airflow pattern provided by the line brattice ventilation system varies with the variation in the associated system drivers. It is important to monitor the quality of ventilation to avoid build-up of methane and accidents.

Hence, the correct option is (B).

78. An airlock is a device that permits the passage of people and objects between a pressure vessel and its surroundings while minimizing the change of pressure in the vessel and loss of air from it. The lock consists of a small chamber with two airtight doors in series which do not open simultaneously.

Hence, the correct option is (D).

79. To detect oxygen-deficient atmosphere teams will use an oxygen indicator.

Flame safety lamps were introduced early in the nineteenth century for the purposes of providing illumination from an oil flame without igniting a methane-air mixture. Their use for illumination disappeared with the development of electric battery lamps. However, the devices were retained for the purposes of testing for methane and oxygen deficiency.

Hence, the correct option is (C).

80. In some mines, carbon dioxide is liberated from the mine roof. Carbon dioxide is a gas formed in a variety of ways. It is a major product of combustion. Normally, it is liberated by micro-organisms oxidizing coal or by mixing acidic mine water with calcium carbonate, found either in surrounding strata or in rock dust.

Hence, the correct option is (B).

81. A Tractor is a self-propelled machine that is used mainly to exert a powerful tractive force for pulling other machines.

The tractor is used for agriculture operations.it can be easily converted to serve as a bulldozer, angle dozer, etc. It is capable of producing a high tractive force.

Hence, the correct option is (A).

82. A grader is used to level the ground and spreads the loose material.

The grader is self-propelled at home by a tractor. It consists of a 3 to 4 M long angled blade supported on a Framework mounted on wheels. It performs various operations like grading, spreading, side cutting and mixing materials.

Hence, the correct option is (C).

83. Material handling is the movement, protection, storage and control of materials and products throughout manufacturing, warehousing, distribution, consumption and disposal. As a process, material handling incorporates a wide range of manual, semi-automated and automated equipment and systems that support logistics and make the supply chain work.

Hence, the correct option is (D).

84. Material handling is the movement, protection, storage and control of materials and products throughout manufacturing, warehousing, distribution, consumption and disposal. As a process, material handling incorporates a wide range of manual, semi-automated and automated equipment and systems that support logistics and make the supply chain work. A company's material handling system and processes are put in place to improve customer service, reduce inventory, shorten delivery time, and lower overall handling costs in manufacturing, distribution and transportation.

Hence, the correct option is (D).

85. Principle of Unit Load states that "it is quicker and economical to move a lot of items at a time rather move each one of them individually". In other words, this principle suggested that the larger the load handled, the lower the cost per unit handled.

Hence, the correct option is (A).

86. Hygiene or maintenance factors are context factors. They provide a background on which people work. They create an atmosphere for doing work, but there is nothing that would motivate them. According to Herzberg, they can dissatisfy by their absence but they cannot satisfy by their presence.

Maintenance factors include status, job security, salary, fringe benefits, work conditions, good pay, paid insurance, vacations.

Hence, the correct option is (A).

87. Type of surveying in which the mean surface of the earth is considered as a plane and the spheroidal shape is neglected called as plane surveying. Plane surveying is a specific type of surveying where the surface of the earth is considered as a plane and the curvature of the earth is not taken into account. The line connecting any two points is a straight line and the angles of polygons are plane angles.

Hence, the correct option is (D).

88. Type of surveying in which the shape of the earth taking into account is geodetic surveying. Geodesists must accurately define the coordinates of points on the surface of the Earth in a consistent manner. A set of accurately measured points is the basis for the National Spatial Reference System, which allows different kinds of maps to be consistent with one another.

Hence, the correct option is (C).

89. The horizontal projection of an area and shows only horizontal distances of the points is a plan or map. Finding the elevations of a point with respect to a given or assumed and establish points given elevation or at different elevations with respect to given or assumed dictum is leveling.

Hence, the correct option is (D).

90. Determining the absolute location of any point or the absolute location and direction of any line on the surface of the earth is called astronomical surveying. An astronomical survey is a general map or image of a region of the sky that lacks a specific observational target. Alternatively, an astronomical survey may comprise a set of many images or spectra of objects that share a common type or feature.

Hence, the correct option is (B).

91. As per the National Building Code, the scale for the Layout plan is specified as 1:500. In this plan, the location of all proposed and existing roads, dimensions of the plot along with building line, locations of sewer and drainage line, etc. are mandatory.

Hence, the correct option is (B).

92. The plan includes floor plans which show the use or occupancy of all parts of the building. Hence these parts need to be large enough for the engineers to understand well. Therefore NBC has a specified scale of 1:100.

Hence, the correct option is (C).

93. A building line usually parallels the plot boundaries and laid down in each case by the Authority, beyond which nothing can be constructed towards the site boundaries.

A Building line or Setback is provided to avoid traffic congestion in front of the building. Buildings like a mall, multi-complexes, factories, etc. which attract a large number of vehicles, should have been set-back a further distance apart from the building line. This line after this extra margin is called as Control Line.

Hence, the correct option is (A).

94. The ratio of the total floor area inclusive of all the floors to the area of the plot on which the building stands is known as the built-up area.

It is also known as the Floor Space Index (FSI) or Floor Area Ratio (FAR). The value of the built-up area is determined by local authorities and it may be different for different areas for different buildings of the town. Floor area means built-up area excluding the area of walls.

Hence, the correct option is (D).

95. A survey station is a prominent point on the chain line and can be either at the beginning of the chain line or at the end. Such a station is known as the Main station.

Hence, the correct option is (C).

96. The book in which the chain or tape measurements are entered is called the field book. It is an oblong book of size about 20 cm x 20 cm and opens lengthwise.

It is of two types:

1.Single line field-book,

2.Double line filed-book.

Hence, the correct option is (C).

97. The chain line may be represented either by a single line or by two lines spaced about 1.5 to 2 cm apart.

Chain lines can be used as central lines, lines of symmetry and trajectories.

Hence, the correct option is (A).

98. At the beginning of a particular survey, the following details must be given, date of survey and names of surveyors, a general sketch of the layout of survey lines, details of survey lines, page index of survey lines, location sketches of survey lines.

Hence, the correct option is (D).

99. Modern GPS surveying can be affected by atmospheric conditions. It can produce more accuracy in its output when compared to pseudo ranging method. This method costs more and is effective for engineering applications.
Hence, the correct option is (A).

100. The position of an object in GPS using pseudo ranging can be done by the calculation time of travel of the signal.

Application of pseudo ranging involves computing distance between GPS antenna and satellite by the correlation between transmitted code and reference code. It needs synchronization between transmitter and receiver clock signal.

Hence, the correct option is (B).

Mock Test 02

General knowledge And Current Affairs

Q.1 What was the theme of International Girls in ICT Day 2022 which is observed annually on the fourth Thursday in April?

A. Access and safety
B. Inspiring the Next Generation
C. Case For Change, Connected Women, IoT and Tech4Girls
D. Powering Change: Women in Innovation and Creativity

Q.2 The Treaty of Mangalore was signed between:

A. The English East India Company and Haidar Ali
B. The English East India Company and Tipu Sultan
C. Haidar Ali and the Zamorin of Calicut
D. The French East India Company and Tipu Sultan

Q.3 The percentage of irrigated land in India is about:

A. 45 **B.** 65 **C.** 35 **D.** 25

Q.4 Which bank is to acquire shares in CSC e-Governance for Rs 36 crores?

A. ICICI **B.** YES Bank
C. AXIS Bank **D.** HDFC Bank

Q.5 Which Indian observatory has become the 3rd IEEE milestone facility?

A. 3.6 m Devasthal Optical Telescope
B. Gauribidanur Radio Observatory
C. Girawali Observatory
D. Giant Metrewave Radio Telescope

Q.6 Which company has signed a pact with NSIL to launch India's first private remote sensing satellite?

A. Pixxel **B.** Blue Origin
C. Virgin Galactic **D.** Bigelow Aerospace

Q.7 The government aims to gradually increase the public health expenditure to what percent of Gross Domestic Product by 2025?

A. 1.5% **B.** 3.5% **C.** 4.5% **D.** 2.5%

Q.8 The national flag was adopted by the Constituent Assembly of India on 22 July 1947 and was presented to the nation at the midnight session of the Assembly on 14th August 1947 on behalf of:

A. The minorities of India
B. The National Integration Council
C. The women of India
D. The people of India

Q.9 Who invented the Ballpoint pen?

A. Biro Brothers **B.** Waterman Brothers
C. Bicc Brothers **D.** Write Brothers

Q.10 Which Indian company has acquired 80% stocks of Big Basket?

A. Reliance Industries
B. Tata Group
C. Indian Oil Corporation
D. Hindustan Petroleum Corporation

Mine management, Legislation and General Safety

Q.11 A major problem with a taskforce type of management is _____

A. There is no logical basis for task force information
B. Its status is too inflexible
C. Accountability
D. Lack of planning

Q.12 Individuals such as Albert Einstein, Edwin Land, and Steven Jobs lead through which type of power?

A. Legitimate **B.** Reward
C. Expert **D.** Charismatic

Q.13 Strategic thinking is a_________process.

A. Short term **B.** Long term
C. Continuous **D.** All of the above

Q.14 Functional managers are responsible _____

A. For a single area of activity
B. To the upper level of management and staff
C. For complex organizational sub-units
D. For obtaining copyrights and patents for newly developed processes and equipment

Q.15 Which one of the following techniques is used for determining allowances in time study?

A. Acceptance sampling
B. Linear regression
C. Performance rating
D. Work sampling

Q.16 Policies are sometimes defined as a(n):

A. Shortcut for thinking
B. Action plan
C. Substitute for strategy
D. Substitute for management authority

Q.17 Which one of the following chart gives simultaneously information about the progress of work and machine loading?

A. Process chart **B.** Machine load chart
C. Man-machine chart **D.** Gantt chart

Q.18 Routing is essential in the following type of industry:

A. Assembly industry
B. Process industry

C. Job order industry
D. Mass production industry

Q.19 The concept of Financial management is:
A. Profit maximization
B. All features of obtaining and using financial resources for company operations
C. Organization of funds
D. Effective management of every company

Q.20 The simplification principle in the material handling method deals with:
A. Make optimum use of equipment
B. Eliminate obstacles from materials flow
C. Integrate operations into handling systems
D. Reduce, combine or eliminate unnecessary movement

Q.21 Unit load principle deals with:
A. Select lightweight material
B. Provide good housekeeping
C. Select a versatile equipment
D. Increase quantity, size, and weight of loads

Q.22 Idle time principle is similar to:
A. Deadweight principle
B. Standardization principle
C. Safety principle
D. Motion principle

Q.23 Which of the following is\are the phase\phases of project management?
A. Project planning **B.** Project scheduling
C. Project controlling **D.** All of the Above

Q.24 Who introduced the bar charts?
A. William Playfair **B.** Henry Gantt
C. Jane Gantt **D.** Joseph Henry

Q.25 The primary purpose of the employee safety program is to preserve the employees':
A. Mental health **B.** Physical health
C. Emotional health **D.** All of the above

Q.26 The visual presentation of the ranking of work sites in a factory based on the number of accidents reported from each site is called:
A. Accident frequency method
B. Spot map method
C. Incidence rate
D. Severity rate

Q.27 Recruitment in coal India is done by which the following methods:
A. Campus Selection
B. All India written test
C. Departmental selection
D. All of the above

Q.28 An E-3 grade officer of excavation discipline is designated as:
A. Executive Engineer **B.** Executive Manager
C. Assistant Manager **D.** All of the above

Q.29 Senior Manager (Civil) is of the following grade:
A. E-5 **B.** E-7
C. E-6 **D.** All of the above

Q.30 EER stands for:
A. Evaluation report of executive
B. Enquiry report of executive
C. Environment Evaluation Report
D. All of the above

Q.31 If the number of males employed in the mine is 253 then the number of latrines required is:
A. 4 **B.** 5 **C.** 6 **D.** 7

Q.32 If the number of persons employed in the mine is 500 then the quantity of water required is:
A. 1000 lit. **B.** 500 lit. **C.** 250 lit. **D.** 1500 lit.

Q.33 What is an electrical schedule?
A. The list or a plan of a building providing information about the number of points in each room
B. The list of all the electrical components required for a particular room
C. The list of electrical components along with their prices
D. Both (B) and (C)

Q.34 What percentage is the incidental charge?
A. 10 % **B.** 5 % **C.** 12 % **D.** 2 %

Q.35 As per the Factories Act, "Adult" means a person who has completed .... year of age.
A. Fifteenth **B.** Sixteenth
C. Seventeenth **D.** Eighteenth

Q.36 As per The Factories Act, "Child" means a person who has not completed his ....year of age.
A. Fourteenth **B.** Fifteenth
C. Sixteenth **D.** Eighteenth

Q.37 Under the OSH Act, employers are responsible for providing a ________
A. Safe workplace **B.** Land
C. Insurance **D.** Estimation

Q.38 OSHA was created to ________
A. Data analysis
B. To reduce hazards
C. Ecological development
D. EIA analysis

Q.39 What is the main purpose of hazard identification?
A. To minimize the effect of a consequence
B. For better risk management
C. To characterize the adverse effect of toxins
D. To reduce the probability of occurrence

Q.40 The information regarding the equipment of the first aid room ismaintained in?

A. First schedule
B. Second schedule
C. Third schedule
D. Fourth schedule

Winning and Working

Q.41 Which of the following is not true about a mineral?
A. Naturally occurring
B. Inorganic substance
C. Organic substance
D. Definite chemical composition

Q.42 Mineralogy deals with:
A. Individual properties of minerals
B. Formation of minerals
C. More of occurrence
D. Properties, formation and occurrence

Q.43 Which of the following rock systems in India is the main source of coal deposits?
A. Dharwar system
B. Vindhyan system
C. Gondwana rock system
D. Cuddapah system

Q.44 In which one of the following types of coal, the higher percentage of carbon is found?
A. Anthracite coal
B. Lignite coal
C. Peat coal
D. Bituminous coal

Q.45 What is the chemical composition of Quartz?
A. SiO_4
B. Si_2O_3
C. SiO_2
D. Al_2O_3

Q.46 Which quartz mineral shows blue color?
A. Rose quartz
B. Blue quartz
C. Smoky quartz
D. Rock crystal

Q.47 Grab sampling consists of:
A. Picking pieces of ore at one place only
B. Picking pieces of ore at random to make up a sample
C. Picking pieces of coal only
D. Picking pieces of ore in a grid fashion

Q.48 The spacing of the trenches, pits, and boreholes depends on:
A. The length of the ore body
B. The modes of occurrence of the deposits
C. The depth of the deposits
D. The outcrops of the deposits

Q.49 The provisions of Sec. 46 of the Factories Act, 1948 impose a statutory obligation on the Railway Administrations to provide and maintain canteens in Railway Establishments, which are governed by the Factories Act and employ more than__________persons.
A. 100
B. 150
C. 250
D. 500

Q.50 In the absence of statutory requirements, the employers may not provide even the basic facilities to the employees. This is the basic assumption of the:
A. Religious theory
B. Policing theory
C. Appeasement theory
D. Benevolence theory

Q.51 The statutory form for keeping the employee's details under the mines act is:
A. Form "K"
B. Form "M"
C. Form "B"
D. None of the above

Q.52 In percussive drilling, the rock is broken by the following action:
A. Crushing
B. Chipping
C. Both
D. None of the above

Q.53 The drilling rods are made of:
A. Castiron
B. Steel
C. Ni-Cr
D. Cast-steel

Q.54 Which of the following method is not used for the holding tool?
A. By a sleeve
B. By chucks
C. By a socket
D. By a lever

Q.55 Which is used for raising and lowering the rods of circular section?
A. Bulldog
B. Sludger
C. Core barrel
D. Retaining key

Q.56 The sludge or cuttings in the borehole are removed with help of:
A. Core barrel
B. Sludger
C. Training key
D. Bulldog

Q.57 A vehicle transporting explosives shall not be driven at a speed exceeding:
A. 25 km/h
B. 20 km/h
C. 15 km/h
D. 30 km/h

Q.58 A cost that is not easily or conveniently traceable to a cost object is known as:
A. Collective cost
B. Indirect cost
C. Additional cost
D. Conversion cost

Q.59 Up to which point on the stress-strain curve is Hooke's law valid?
A. Elastic limit
B. Yield point
C. Proportionality limit
D. Fracture point

Q.60 What is the unit for stress?
A. N/m^2
B. Nm^2
C. N/m
D. Nm

Surface environment, Mine Ventilation and Hazards

Q.61 What is essential in an EIA?
A. It allows decision-makers to assess a project's impacts in all its phases.
B. It allows the public and other stakeholders to present their views and inputs on the planned development.

C. It contributes to and improves the project design, so that environmental, as well as socioeconomic measures, are core parts of it.
D. All of the above

Q.62 What is not a key step in developing an EMP?

1. Summary of the potential impacts of the proposal.
2. A review of EIA legislation in 5 different countries.
3. Description of the recommended mitigation measures.
4. Statement of their compliance with relevant standards.
5. Allocation of resources and response
6. Program for monitoring and auditing.
7. Abilities for plan implementation.
8. Schedule of the actions to be taken.

A. 6 **B.** 7
C. 2 **D.** None of the above

Q.63 ________ represents the heavier inert matter in wastewater.
A. Debris **B.** Waste **C.** Screens **D.** Grit

Q.64 ____ devices remove materials that would damage equipment or interfere with a process.
A. Grit **B.** Screening
C. Oxidation **D.** Reduction

Q.65 Which is the first state in India to make rooftop rainwater harvesting compulsory to all the houses?
A. Tamil Nadu **B.** Kerala
C. Assam **D.** Goa

Q.66 The name given to the diversion channels of the western Himalayas is______________
A. Phalodi **B.** Johads
C. Guls or Kuls **D.** None of these

Q.67 What is meant by the term "black damp"?
A. An atmosphere sufficient in oxygen
B. An atmosphere deficient in oxygen
C. An atmosphere deficient in nitrogen
D. An atmosphere sufficient in nitrogen

Q.68 How can methane gas be detected in a coal mine?
A. Chemical analysis **B.** Flame safety lamp
C. Methane detectors **D.** All of the above

Q.69 How many types of gases are found in underground mines leaving O_2 , N_2 , CO_2 normal gas?
A. 5 **B.** 7
C. 9 **D.** None of these

Q.70 Which gas is found after the explosion in mines?
A. CH_4 **B.** H_2S
C. Gob stink **D.** After Damp

Q.71 For the separation of which of the following substances, Gas-solid chromatography is being used?
A. Thermally stable organic components
B. Volatile organic components
C. Thermally stable inorganic components
D. Low molecular weight gaseous species

Q.72 Which of the following is not a feature of carrier gas used in gas chromatography?
A. It must be chemically inert
B. It should be suitable for the detector employed
C. It should not be completely pure
D. It should be cheap

Q.73 The TLV for carbon dioxide is ___________.
A. 15.0% **B.** 10.0% **C.** 5.0% **D.** 0.5%

Q.74 An anemometer actually measures ___________ of air.
A. Linear feet of travel **B.** Quantity
C. Velocity **D.** All of the above

Q.75 What is the role of breaker house in coal feeding?
A. To break the coal into smaller pieces
B. To separate different sizes of coal
C. To separate the light dust from the coal
D. To powder the coal

Q.76 When coal is being burnt how much % of ash is formed compared to the whole amount?
A. 10-20% **B.** 40-50% **C.** 25-35% **D.** 4-10%

Q.77 Why is it important to prefer ash handling systems?
A. Coal ash produced annually is very less
B. Coal ash produced annually accounts for thousands of tonnes
C. Coal ash can be reutilized for some other purpose
D. Coal ash affects the health of people working at plants

Q.78 To detect oxygen ________ atmospheres teams will use an ________ indicator.
A. Poor, hydrogen **B.** Enriched, methane
C. Deficient, oxygen **D.** None of the above

Q.79 In some mines, carbon dioxide is liberated from the ______________.
A. Rock strata **B.** Mine roof
C. Mine floor **D.** None of the above

Q.80 __________ can be _________ with a multi-gas detector or by chemical analysis.
A. Methane, found **B.** Hydrogen, detected
C. Oxygen, detected **D.** None of these

Mine Machineries, surveying and electricity

Q.81 Which of the following types of fiber rope offers the best uniform strength and service?
A. Manila **B.** Polyester
C. Henequen **D.** Polypropylene

Q.82 The Forklift truck is used for:

A. Lifting and lowering
B. Vertical transportation
C. Both (A) and (B)
D. None of the above

Q.83 Wheelbarrows are used for:

A. Lifting and lowering
B. Vertical transportation
C. Both (A) and (B)
D. None of the above

Q.84 Cranes are used for:

A. Lifting and lowering
B. Vertical transportation
C. Both (A) and (B)
D. None of the above

Q.85 Which of the following is the correct classification of pumps?

A. Physical principle of operation
B. Mechanical principle of operation
C. Chemical principle of operation
D. Biological principle of operation

Q.86 Displacement pump is classified on the basis of __________

A. Principle of Mechanical Operation
B. Type of power
C. Type of service
D. Efficiency

Q.87 What is the advantage of sectionalizing the power plant?

A. High reliability **B.** Low capital cost
C. Low maintenance **D.** Easy operation

Q.88 Which of the following is equal to the maximum demand?

A. The ratio of area under the curve to the total area of the rectangle
B. The ratio of area under curve and number of hours
C. The peak of the load curve
D. The area under the curve

Q.89 Fujairah is a free trade zone located in:

A. Dubai **B.** Sharjah **C.** Mumbai **D.** Cairo

Q.90 Direct payments made by the government to domestic companies to encourage exports or to protect them from imports are known as:

A. Voluntary export restraints
B. Subsidies
C. Export tariffs
D. Aids

Q.91 The area under the load curve represents __________

A. The average load on the power system
B. Maximum demand
C. Number of units generated
D. Load factor

Q.92 The main function of a fuse is to:

A. Protect the line
B. Open the circuit
C. Prevent excessive currents
D. None of the above

Q.93 On which of the following routine tests are conducted?

A. Oil circuit breakers
B. Airblast circuit breakers
C. Minimum oil circuit breakers
D. All of the above

Q.94 A silicon controlled rectifier (SCR) is a:

A. Unijunction device
B. Device with three junction
C. Device with four junction
D. None of the above

Q.95 A Thyristor is basically:

A. PNPN device
B. A combination of diac and triac
C. A set of SCRs
D. None of the above

Q.96 Determining the relative positions of points above or beneath the surface of the earth by means of direct or indirect measurements of distance and direction and elevation is called ________.

A. Surveying **B.** Leveling
C. Measuring **D.** Contouring

Q.97 Which branch of surveying is used to find the elevations of given points with respect to given or assumed datum?

A. Levelling
B. Contouring
C. Traversing
D. Plane table surveying

Q.98 In order to form a normal equation __________ are needed.

A. Algebraic coefficients
B. Probability equations
C. Probability laws
D. Probability curves

Q.99 Correlates can also be known as __________

A. Unknown multiples **B.** Known multiples
C. Eccentric multiples **D.** Centric multiples

Q.100 All conditions are to be collected and used in which of the following case?

A. Most probable value
B. Normal equation
C. Method of correlates
D. Probability law

// Smart Answer Sheet //

Correct Percentage of students who answered correctly. **Skipped** Percentage of students who skipped.

Q.	Ans.	Correct	Skipped	Q.	Ans.	Correct	Skipped	Q.	Ans.	Correct	Skipped	Q.	Ans.	Correct	Skipped	Q.	Ans.	Correct	Skipped	Q.	Ans.	Correct	Skipped
1	A	78.49 %	0.0 %	18	A	40.52 %	1.08 %	35	D	86.33 %	0.0 %	52	B	51.15 %	1.88 %	69	C	19.37 %	4.78 %	86	A	45.72 %	1.86 %
2	B	76.26 %	0.0 %	19	B	61.05 %	1.18 %	36	B	79.48 %	0.0 %	53	C	76.76 %	0.0 %	70	D	59.96 %	1.38 %	87	A	67.08 %	1.58 %
3	C	68.08 %	1.52 %	20	D	54.18 %	1.29 %	37	A	59.84 %	1.45 %	54	D	53.95 %	1.97 %	71	D	53.11 %	1.23 %	88	C	31.87 %	4.02 %
4	C	68.96 %	1.35 %	21	D	68.36 %	1.02 %	38	B	69.81 %	1.17 %	55	A	63.73 %	1.38 %	72	C	67.11 %	1.2 %	89	A	58.52 %	1.9 %
5	D	62.82 %	1.52 %	22	D	29.57 %	4.14 %	39	C	77.45 %	0.0 %	56	B	40.54 %	1.63 %	73	D	55.32 %	1.63 %	90	B	52.22 %	1.77 %
6	A	57.31 %	1.89 %	23	D	86.81 %	0.0 %	40	B	58.09 %	1.99 %	57	A	47.38 %	1.79 %	74	C	63.73 %	1.18 %	91	C	66.56 %	1.28 %
7	D	56.76 %	1.21 %	24	A	30.89 %	3.97 %	41	C	45.1 %	1.39 %	58	B	63.45 %	1.05 %	75	C	46.81 %	1.61 %	92	C	67.97 %	1.63 %
8	C	43.86 %	1.42 %	25	D	43.26 %	1.68 %	42	D	69.1 %	1.08 %	59	C	87.55 %	0.0 %	76	A	29.48 %	3.68 %	93	D	50.23 %	1.21 %
9	A	53.19 %	1.13 %	26	B	15.57 %	3.83 %	43	C	63.71 %	1.16 %	60	A	80.94 %	0.0 %	77	B	46.67 %	1.63 %	94	B	32.95 %	4.85 %
10	B	78.24 %	0.0 %	27	D	84.08 %	0.0 %	44	A	85.98 %	0.0 %	61	D	88.97 %	0.0 %	78	C	67.5 %	1.42 %	95	A	52.75 %	1.33 %
11	B	81.93 %	0.0 %	28	C	59.84 %	1.16 %	45	C	69.97 %	1.7 %	62	C	87.48 %	0.0 %	79	B	80.37 %	0.0 %	96	A	58.26 %	1.84 %
12	C	76.27 %	0.0 %	29	C	54.89 %	1.36 %	46	B	43.26 %	1.92 %	63	D	47.26 %	1.92 %	80	B	60.95 %	1.54 %	97	A	52.88 %	1.99 %
13	C	79.17 %	0.0 %	30	C	68.37 %	1.04 %	47	B	69.56 %	1.94 %	64	B	63.78 %	1.78 %	81	A	67.89 %	1.23 %	98	A	58.78 %	1.41 %
14	A	84.96 %	0.0 %	31	C	11.67 %	3.51 %	48	B	21.63 %	3.02 %	65	A	46.33 %	1.78 %	82	C	44.29 %	1.4 %	99	A	29.17 %	4.87 %
15	D	63.76 %	1.89 %	32	A	43.99 %	1.91 %	49	C	60.38 %	1.37 %	66	C	32.94 %	3.23 %	83	A	57.44 %	1.98 %	100	C	56.78 %	1.02 %
16	D	61.57 %	1.51 %	33	A	67.69 %	1.16 %	50	B	57.11 %	1.64 %	67	B	53.56 %	1.9 %	84	C	40.06 %	1.59 %				
17	C	89.63 %	0.0 %	34	B	68.63 %	1.09 %	51	C	57.12 %	1.14 %	68	D	48.61 %	1.54 %	85	B	13.12 %	4.5 %				

//Hints and Solutions//

1. The theme of International Girls in ICT Day 2022 was Access and Safety. It is celebrated every year on the fourth Thursday in April. International Girls in ICT Day aims to inspire a global movement to increase the representation of girls and women in technology.

Hence, the correct option is (A).

2. The Treaty of Mangalore was signed between Tipu Sultan and the English East India Company on 11 March 1784. It was signed in Mangalore and brought an end to the Second Anglo-Mysore War.

Hence, the correct option is (B).

3. Irrigation in India includes both major and minor canals from Indian rivers, tanks, and other rainwater harvesting projects for agricultural activities. The Economic Survey of 2018 states that agriculture in India even today relies heavily on the weather because the percentage of irrigated land in India is 35% as per the survey.

Hence, the correct option is (C).

4. Axis Bank has acquired over 57,700 shares in CSC e-Governance Services India Ltd for Rs 36 crores. Axis Bank has executed a pact for subscribing to 57,743 equity shares of a face value of Rs 1000 each to be issued by CSC e-Governance Services India Ltd at Rs 6,300 per equity share.

Hence, the correct option is (C).

5. The Giant Metrewave Radio Telescope (GMRT), one of the world's largest and low-frequency radio observatories, has been selected as an Institute of Electrical and Electronics Engineers (IEEE) Milestone facility. Giant Metrewave Radio Telescope (GMRT) has become the third Indian scientific facility to be awarded the Institute of Electrical and Electronics Engineers (IEEE) milestone for its novel engineering, advanced technology, and scientific contributions made in the field of radio astronomy. A very special telescope - GMRT - designed, built, and operated by Indian scientists and engineers. It is used by radio astronomers from across the world to study our Universe.

Hence, the correct option is (D).

6. Space start-up Pixxel has signed an agreement with State-run New Space India Limited (NSIL) to launch the country's first private remote-sensing satellite on an ISRO PSLV rocket in early 2021.

The agreement is one of its kind after the establishment of IN-SPACe, the authorization and regulatory body under the Department of Space for enabling private players to undertake space activities in India.

Hence, the correct option is (A).

7. India is set to increase its public health spending to 2.5 percent of its gross domestic product (GDP) by 2025. Prime Minister Narendra Modi said that women, children, and the youth will continue to remain at the heart of every policy, program, and initiative of the government. Addressing the 2018 Partners' Forum, Modi said the high out-of-pocket expenditure incurred by families to avail medical care in India worried his government, and to address the issue they launched the Ayushman Bharat Yojana.

Hence, the correct option is (D).

8. The National Flag of India was adopted by the Constituent Assembly on the 22nd July 1947 and presented to the Nation on behalf of the women of India at the mid-night session of the assembly on August 14, 1947.

Presenting the National Flag to the House on behalf of the women of India, Srimati Hansa Mehta said"In the absence of Srimati Sarojini Naidu, it is my proud privilege on behalf of the women of India to present this flag to the nation".

Hence, the correct option is (C).

9. The Hungarian brothers, Laszlo and George Biro made the first Ballpoint pen in 1894. It followed the first workable fountain pen which was invented by L.E. Waterman in 1884.

Hence, the correct option is (A).

10. The Tata Group has entered advanced talks to buy as much as 80 percent stake of Alibaba-backed online grocer Big Basket for $1.3 billion. After the deal, the local online grocer will see its value soar to $1.6 billion.

Hence, the correct option is (B).

11. A major problem with a taskforce type of management is that it's too inflexible. Taskforce is a type of group, formed temporarily, in which people from different disciplinary backgrounds come together to perform a specific task or mission. These are different from the committees in the sense, these are temporary and have broader powers of action and decision, greater responsibilities for investigation, analysis, planning, and research.

Hence, the correct option is (B).

12. Albert Einstein, Edwin Land, and Steven Jobs are scientists and inventors who have expertise in their area of interest.

Albert Einstein has a clear view of the problems of physics and the determination to solve them.

Edwin Herbert Land American inventor and physicist whose one-step process for developing and printing photographs culminated in a revolution in photography unparalleled since the advent of roll film.

Steven Paul Jobs was an American inventor, designer, and entrepreneur who was the co-founder, chief executive, and chairman of Apple Computer. Apple's revolutionary products, which include the iPod, iPhone, and iPad, are now seen as dictating the evolution of modern technology.

Hence, the correct option is (C).

13. Strategic thinking is a continuous process. Strategic thinking is the ability to plan for the future. It's the capacity to prepare strategies and conjure ideas that will both cope with changing environments and consider the various challenges that lie ahead.

Hence, the correct option is (C).

14. Functional managers are responsible for a single area of activity. A functional manager manages and owns the resources in a specific department, such as IT, engineering, public relations, or marketing, and generally directs the technical work of individuals from that functional area who are working on the project.

Hence, the correct option is (A).

15. Work sampling techniques are used for determining allowances in time study.

Work sampling is a method in which a large number of instantaneous observations are made at random time intervals over a period of time or a group of machines, workers, or processes/operations. Each observation records what is happening at that instant and the percentage of observations recorded for a particular activity or delay/idleness is a measure of the percentage of time during which that activity or delay/idleness occurs.

Hence, the correct option is (D).

16. Policies are sometimes defined as a substitute for management authority.

A policy is a set of ideas or plans that is used as a basis for making decisions, especially in politics, economics, or business.

Hence, the correct option is (D).

17. The Man-machine chart gives simultaneously information about the progress of work and machine loading. A man-machine chart graphically represents the relationship between the manual work performed by one or more operators and one or more machines involved in a manufacturing process.

It is typically used to plan the activity of resources in large and medium series.

Each resource continually performs the same tasks. When the last task is completed, the resource runs again the first task. This estate is called a cycle. A diagram is constituted of tangled cycles. The duration of the longest cycle is called the time of the cycle. It is usually the time needed to produce or assemble a piece.

Hence, the correct option is (C).

18. Routing is essential in the assembling industry.

Routing is the process of selecting a path for traffic in a network or between or across multiple networks.

Assembly industries are engaged in bringing together various components or parts of bicycles, television, radio and these are some examples of assembling industries.

Hence, the correct option is (A).

19. The concept of Financial management deals with the all features of obtaining and using financial resources for company operations. Financial Management means planning, organizing, directing, and controlling the financial activities such as procurement and utilization of funds of the enterprise. It means applying general management principles to the financial resources of the enterprise.

Hence, the correct option is (B).

20. The simplification principle in the material handling method deals with the reduce, combine, or eliminate unnecessary movement.

Reduce, combine, or eliminate unnecessary movement and/or equipment increases the efficiency in materials handling.

Hence, the correct option is (D).

21. The Unit load principle deals with increase quantity, size, the weight of loads handled.

A unit load is the amount of material that can be moved as a single mass between two locations. The Primary advantage of using unit loads is the Capability of handling more items at a time and reducing the number of trips, handling cost, loading and unloading times, and product damage.

Hence, the correct option is (D).

22. The Idle time principle reduces the idle or unproductive time of both materials handling equipment and manpower. This principle is similar to the motion principle, so far as materials handling equipment are concerned.

Hence, the correct option is (D).

23. There are three phases of project management.

These are project planning, project scheduling, and project controlling.

Project management refers to a highly specialized job to achieve the objectives of a project.

Hence, the correct option is (D).

24. William Playfair is generally considered to have introduced the bar chart in a graph titled "Exports and Imports of Scotland to and from different parts for one Year from Christmas 1780 to Christmas 1781".

Hence, the correct option is (A).

25. The primary purpose of an employee safety program is to preserve the employees':

- Mental health
- Physical health
- Emotional health

A health and safety program is a definite plan of action designed to prevent accidents and occupational diseases. A health and safety program must include the elements required by the health and safety legislation.

Hence, the correct option is (D).

26. The visual presentation of the ranking of work sites in a factory based on the number of accidents reported from each site is called the spot map method.

A method of displaying the geographical distribution of a disease, sometimes helpful in the epidemic investigation, in which cases of a disease of interest are plotted on a map. From the distribution, it may be possible to make inferences about the origin of a point-source epidemic and its mode of spread and thus initiate suitable control measures.

Hence, the correct option is (B).

27. Coal India Limited (CIL) is an Indian public sector coal mining and refining company headquartered in Kolkata, West Bengal. It is the largest coal-producing company in the world and a Maharatna public sector undertaking.

Recruitment in coal India is done by all of these methods:

- Campus Selection
- All India written test
- Departmental selection

Hence, the correct option is (D).

28. An E-3 grade officer of excavation discipline is designated as assistant manager (Excv).

These are the hierarchy level for executive cadre in PSUs.

Grades and Designations

E-1	Fresh recruitment -Management trainee/ Deptt candidate - Officer
E-2	Sr. Officer (Discipline/Statutory designation if any)
E-3	Asstt Manager(Discipline/Statutory designation if any)
E-4	Deputy Manager(Discipline/Statutory designation if any)
E-5	Manager(Discipline/Statutory designation if any)
E-6	Sr.Manager(Discipline/statutory designation if any)
E-7	Chief Manager(Discipline/Statutory designation if any)
E-8	General Manager(Discipline/Statutory designation if any)
E-9	Executive Director (Discipline/statutory designation if any)

Hence, the correct option is (C).

29. Senior Manager (Civil) is of E-6 grade.

These are the hierarchy level for the executive cadre in PSU:

Grades and Designation

E-1	Fresh recruitment -Management trainee/ Deptt candidate Officer
E-2	Sr. Officer (Discipline/Statutory designation if any)
E-3	Asstt Manager(Discipline/Statutory designation if any)
E-4	Deputy Manager(Discipline/Statutory designation if any)
E-5	Manager(Discipline/Statutory designation if any)
E-6	Sr.Manager(Discipline/statutory designation if any)
E-7	Chief Manager(Discipline/Statutory designation if any)
E-8	General Manager(Discipline/Statutory designation if any)
E-9	Executive Director (Discipline/statutory designation if any)

Hence, the correct option is (C).

30. EER stands for Environment Evaluation Report.

EER is concerned with an already impacted environment as it concerns in relation to an existing project or activity. EER serves as an important tool that enables policymakers to know the state of the impacted environment in relation to those actions not subjected to EIA at the pre-planning or preliminary stage. This is with a view to deciding the appropriate and design strategies for the protection and restoration of the particular environment.

Hence, the correct option is (C).

31. If the number of males employed in the mine is 253 then the number of latrines required is 6.

(1) There shall be provided, separately for males and females in every mine, a sufficient number of latrines and urinals of prescribed types so situated as to be convenient and accessible to persons employed in the mine at all times.

(2) All latrines and urinals provided under Mines rules shall be adequately lighted, ventilated, and at all times maintained in a clean and sanitary condition.

(3) The Central Government may specify the number of latrines and urinals to be provided in any mine, in proportion to the number of males and females employed in the mine and provide for such other matters in respect of sanitation in mines (including the obligations) in this regard of persons employed in the mine as it may consider necessary in the interests of the health of the persons so employed.

Hence, the correct option is (C).

32. If the number of persons employed in the mine is 500 then the quantity of water required is 1000 lit.

Quantity of drinking water—

(1) The quantity of drinking water to be provided in a mine or any part thereof shall be on a scale of at least 1[two liters] for every person employed at any one time and such drinking water shall be readily available at conveniently accessible points during the whole of the working shift.

(2) Where 100 persons or more are employed, either above ground or in opencast working, at any one time, an Inspector may by order in writing require the drinking water to be effectively cooled by mechanical or other means available.

(3) No charge shall be made for the drinking water so supplied.

Hence, the correct option is (A).

33. An electrical schedule is a list or a plan of a building providing information about the number of points in each room.

Preparing an electrical schedule helps in determining the amount of power required for an installation. This information is then used by electrical engineers to properly size conductors, conduits and determine the proper overload and other protection and control systems.

Hence, the correct option is (A).

34. Incidental charges are costs of items and services that are not part of the main bill. Incidental expenses, also known as incidentals, are gratuities and other minor fees or costs incurred in addition to the main service, item or event paid for during business activities. 5 % is the incidental charge.

Hence, the correct option is (B).

35. As per the Factories Act, "Adult" means a person who has completed "18" years of age. An adult is a mature, fully developed person. The Adult has reached an age when they are legally responsible for their actions.

Hence, the correct option is (D).

36. As per the Factories Act, "Child" means a person who has not completed his 15 years of age.

According to the Factories Act, 1948 a child is a person who has completed his/her fifteen years of age but has not completed his/her eighteen years are known as an 'adolescent". According to this Act, an adolescent is only allowed to work in a factory between 6 a.m. and 7 p.m.

Hence, the correct option is (B).

37. Under the OSH Act, employers are accountable for providing a safe and healthful workplace. OSHA's mission is to assure safe and healthful workplaces by enforcing standards, and by providing training, outreach, education, and help.OSHA stands for Occupational Safety and Health Administration.

Hence, the correct option is (A).

38. OSHA(Occupational Safety and Health Administration)was created mainly to encourage employees and employers to reduce workplace hazards and to implement safety and health programs. The mission of OSHA is to save lives, prevent injuries, and protect the health of workers, maintaining, reporting, and recordkeeping systems to keep track of job-related injuries and illnesses, and providing training programs to increase knowledge about occupational safety and health.

Hence, the correct option is (B).

39. Hazard identification is the first step in risk assessment. The goal is to understand the concentration of toxins, spatial distribution, and movement.

Hazard identification is part of the process used to evaluate if any particular situation, item, thing, etc. may have the potential to cause harm. The term often used to describe the full process is risk assessment:

Identify hazards and risk factors that have the potential to cause harm (hazard identification).

Analyze and evaluate the risk associated with that hazard (risk analysis, and risk evaluation).

Determine appropriate ways to eliminate the hazard, or control the risk when the hazard cannot be eliminated (risk control).

Overall, the goal of hazard identification is to find and record possible hazards that may be present in your workplace.

Hence, the correct option is (C).

40. The information regarding the equipment of the first aid room is maintained in the second schedule.

Under health and safety (First Aid) regulations 1981, employers must:

- Provide first aid at work
- Tell employees about first aid facilities

The first aid equipment and facilities and trained staff available will depend on:

- The number of employees
- The nature of the work carried out
- The size and type of workplace
- The location of the workplace

Hence, the correct option is (B).

41. A mineral is defined as, a naturally occurring inorganic solid substance that is characterized by definite chemical composition and very often with a definite atomic structure. A mineral is an inorganic substance. It was not made by living organisms. Organic substances contain carbon.

Hence, the correct option is (C).

42. Mineralogy is the branch of geology dealing with the wide range of aspects related to minerals like their individual properties, mode of occurrence, and mode of formation.

Hence, the correct option is (D).

43. Gondwana rock systems in India is the main source of coal deposits.

The Gondwana coal is mainly bituminous or anthracite in which the carbon content varies between 60 to 90 percent. The bituminous coal is converted into coke before being used in the iron and steel industry.

Tertiary coal is found in the rocks of the Oligocene period of the Tertiary Era.

Hence, the correct option is (C).

44. Anthracite has the highest percentage of carbon content.

Anthracite, also known as hard coal. It is a hard, compact variety of coal that has a submetallic luster. It has the highest carbon content, the fewest impurities, and the highest energy density of all types of coal and has the highest-ranking in coals.

Hence, the correct option is (A).

45. The chemical composition of the quartz minerals is SiO_2. In other words, silicon dioxide is the basic chemical composition of the quartz minerals. Quartz is a hard, crystalline mineral composed of silicon and oxygen atoms. The atoms are linked in a continuous framework of SiO_4 silicon-oxygen tetrahedra, with each oxygen being shared between two tetrahedra.

Hence, the correct option is (C).

46. The blue quartz shows a distinct blue color compared to the other quartz minerals.

The color may be caused by the color of the included minerals or by The Rayleigh scattering of light at microscopic inclusions.

Hence, the correct option is (B).

47. Grab sampling consists of picking pieces of ore at random to make up a sample.

A grab sample is an individual sample collected without compositing or adding other samples.

A grab sample is generally appropriate for sampling from smaller facilities.

Hence, the correct option is (B).

48. The spacing of the trenches, pits, and boreholes depends on the modes of occurrence of the deposits.

Borehole Mining (BHM) is a remote operated method of extraction (mining) of mineral resources through boreholes based on the in-situ conversion of ores into a mobile form (slurry) by means of high-pressure water jets (hydraulicking). This process can be carried out from the land surface, open pit floor, underground mine or floating platform, or vessel through pre-drilled boreholes.

Pits are shallow, square-shaped holes while trenches are long, linear, and variable in depth. Rock and soil removed from the trench or pit is stored on site.

Hence, the correct option is (B).

49. According to the provisions of Sec. 46 Factories Act, 1948. The State Government may make rules requiring that in any specified factory wherein more than two hundred and fifty workers are ordinarily employed, a canteen or canteens shall be provided and maintained by the occupier for the use of the workers.

Hence, the correct option is (C).

50. The policing theory is based on the contention that a minimum standard of welfare is necessary for laborers. Apparently, this theory assumes that man is selfish and self-centered, and always tries to achieve his own ends, even at the cost of the welfare of others. The policing theory leads to the passing of laws relating to the provision of minimum welfare for workers. Periodical supervision to ascertain that these welfare measures are provided and implemented and punishment of employers who evade or disobey these laws. In this theory, the emphasis is unfortunately on fear and not on the spirit of welfare, which should be the guiding factor.

Hence, the correct option is (B).

51. The statutory form for keeping the employee's details under the mines act is form "B".

A statutory form is a form created by a government, usually designed to serve as a model form or a free form for the public. The text of the form resides within the government's statutes.

Hence, the correct option is (C).

52. In percussive drilling, the rock is broken by the chipping action. Chipping is a method of sampling a rock exposure whereby a regular series of small chips of rock is broken off along a line across the face.

Percussive drilling is a manual drilling technique in which a heavy cutting or hammering bit attached to a rope or cable is lowered in the open hole or inside a temporary casing. The technique is often also referred to as 'Cable tool'. Usually, a tripod is used to support the tools.

Hence, the correct option is (B).

53. The drilling rods are made of Ni-Cr (Nickel-Chromium). A nickel-chromium alloy with good oxidation resistance at higher temperatures, with good resistance in carburizing and chloride containing environments.

Inconel 600 is a nickel-chromium alloy designed for use from cryogenic to elevated temperatures in the range of 2000 deg F(1093 deg C). The high nickel content of the alloy enables it to retain considerable resistance under reducing conditions and makes it resistant to corrosion by a number of organic and inorganic compounds. The nickel content gives it excellent resistance to chloride-ion stress-corrosion cracking and also provides excellent resistance to alkaline solutions.

Hence, the correct option is (C).

54. A lever is not used for holding tools. A lever is a simple machine made of a rigid beam and a fulcrum. The effort (input force) and load (output force) are applied to either end of the beam.

All other given methods are used for holding tools. There are various types of chucks two jaw chuck, three-jaw chuck, etc. Sleeves and sockets are also used for holding tools.

Hence, the correct option is (D).

55. Bulldog is used for raising and lowering the rods of circular section.

A device known as a retaining key is used at the time of raising or lowering the rods of square cross-section. The same purpose is served in the case of rods of circular cross-section with flush joints, by a device known as "bulldog safety clamp".

Hence, the correct option is (A).

56. The sludge or cuttings in the borehole are removed with help of a sludger. Sludger has a cylinder, with a valve at the end, for removing the sludge from a bore-hole.

Hence, the correct option is (B).

57. A vehicle transporting explosives shall not be driven at a speed exceeding 25 km/h.

Transportation of explosives shall meet the provisions of Department of Transportation regulations.

The regulation provides that a vehicle carrying explosives must not be driven at a speed greater than the maximum applicable speed limit for that road, or the speed which the driver is directed not to exceed by a supervisor.

Hence, the correct option is (A).

58. A cost that is not easily or conveniently traceable to a cost object is known as an indirect cost.

Indirect costs are those costs that cannot be directly associated with a product or service. Although they are often fixed, this is not always the case. They should be controlled by departmental managers and include all costs that are not directly associated with a product or service.

Hence, the correct option is (B).

59. Up to the proportional limit on the stress-strain curve, Hooke's law is valid.

The proportionality limit is the point up to which the strain of an elastic body is proportional to the stress applied to it. While the elastic point is the point up to which the elastic properties last. After fracture point the body breaks.

Hence, the correct option is (C).

60. Stress is basically a force per unit area.

The dimension for force is N and the dimension of the area is m^2. Therefore, the unit for stress is the dimension of force divided by that of the area which is N/m^2.

Hence, the correct option is (A).

61. The essentials points in an EIA (Environmental Impact Assessment)

- It allows decision-makers to assess a project's impacts in all its phases.
- It allows the public and other stakeholders to present their views and inputs on the planned development.
- It contributes to and improves the project design so that environmental as well as socioeconomic measures are core parts of it.

Hence, the correct option is (D).

62. Review of EIA (Environmental Impact Assessment) legislation in 5 different countries, not a key step in developing an EMP(Environment Management Plan).

An Environmental Management Plan (EMP) can be defined as an environmental management tool used to ensure that undue or reasonably avoidable adverse impacts of the construction, operation, and decommissioning of a project are prevented and that the positive benefits of the projects are enhanced.EMPs are therefore important tools for ensuring that the management actions arising from Environmental Impact Assessment (EIA) processes are clearly defined and implemented through all phases of the project life-cycle.

Hence, the correct option is (C).

63. Grit represents the heavier inert matter in wastewater which will not decompose in treatment processes. It is identified with matter having a specific gravity of about 2.65 and the design of grit chambers is based on the removal of all particles of about 0.011 inch or larger.

Hence, the correct option is (D).

64. Screening devices remove materials that would damage equipment or interfere with a process or piece of equipment. Screening devices have a varied application in wastewater treatment facilities.

Hence, the correct option is (B).

65. Tamil Nadu is the first state in India that has made rooftop rainwater harvesting structures compulsory to all the houses across the state. If anyone failed to obey this, there are legal provisions to punish the defaulters. This method helps to save rainwater.

Hence, the correct option is (A).

66. The diversions channels of the western Himalaya is known as Guls or Kuls. In hills and mountains, people built diversion channels for irrigational purposes, which are called Guls and Kuls. It is mainly used in the western Himalayas for harvesting water.

Hence, the correct option is (C).

67. In mine gas, "black damp" is an atmosphere in which a flame lamp will not burn, usually because of an excess of carbon dioxide (CO_2) and nitrogen in the air.

Hence, the correct option is (B).

68. Methane gas can be detected in a coal mine by Chemical analysis, Flame safety lamp, and Methane detectors. Carbon monoxide can be detected by means of carbon monoxide detectors, multigas detectors.

Hence, the correct option is (D).

69. The main toxic gases in mines are carbon monoxide (CO) and carbon dioxide (CO_2).

The flammable gases are methane (CH_4), CO, and hydrogen (H_2).

The suffocating gases are CO_2, nitrogen (N_2), and CH_4.

The toxic gases are CO, nitrogen oxides (NOx), and hydrogen sulfide (H_2S).

The detonation gases are NO_2, nitric oxide (NO), ammonia (NH_3), hydrogen (H_2), carbon monoxide (CO), carbon dioxide (CO_2), nitrogen (N_2), oxygen, (O_2), and methane (CH_4).

Hence, the correct option is (C).

70. Afterdamp is the toxic mixture of gases left in a mine following an explosion caused by firedamp, which itself can initiate a much larger explosion of coal dust. It consists of carbon dioxide, carbon monoxide, and nitrogen.

Hence, the correct option is (D).

71. Gas-solid chromatography is used for the separation of low molecular weight gaseous species. Its application is limited because of the semi-permanent retention of the analyte. Gas-solid distribution is widely employed for purification, using special adsorbents called molecular sieves. These materials contain pores of approximately the same dimensions as small molecules.

Hence, the correct option is (D).

72. The Carrier gas used in gas chromatography should be highly pure. Further, it should be readily available and non-inflammable.

Hence, the correct option is (C).

73. The TLV (Threshold Limit Values) for carbon dioxide is 0.5%. The American Conference of Governmental Industrial Hygienists (ACGIH) Society has established the threshold limit values (TLVs) for various chemical substances and physical agents in order to protect workers by providing timely, objective, scientific information to occupational and environmental health professionals.

TLVs of airborne substances refer to those concentrations within which personnel may be exposed without known adverse effects to their health or safety.

Hence, the correct option is (D).

74. An anemometer is an instrument used to measure the speed or velocity of gases either in a contained flow or in a duct or in unconfined flows, such as atmospheric wind.

Hence, the correct option is (C).

75. The role of breaker house in coal feeding is to separate the light dust from the coal.

Because of the brittle nature of the coal, it is common nature of coal to emit light dust/coal dust during transportation, mining, and machine handling. This dust needs to be cleared out and it is performed by a coal breaker.

Hence, the correct option is (C).

76. 10-20% of ash is formed compared to the whole amount of coal when the coal is burnt.

The coal available in nature already contains some percent of ash, when it is burnt. Due to its brittle nature, more amount of ash is produced, coal is one of the largest types of industrial waste generator. For environmental benefits, this coal ash is reused as a type of by-product in different types of industries.

Hence, the correct option is (A).

77. Considering the large coal-burning capacity plant of modern times, the amount of ash produced when the coal is burnt is in thousands of tonnes. It could have an effect on other subjects too if the proper ash handling methods are not followed. For different environmental, economic, and product benefits the coal ash is reused by different types of industries in different ways of its necessity.

Hence, the correct option is (B).

78. To detect oxygen-deficient atmospheres teams will use an oxygen indicator.

Flame safety lamps were introduced early in the nineteenth century for the purposes of providing illumination from an oil flame without igniting a methane-air mixture. Their use for illumination disappeared with the development of electric battery lamps. However, the devices were retained for the purposes of testing for methane and oxygen deficiency.

Hence, the correct option is (C).

79. In some mines, carbon dioxide is liberated from the mine roof because carbon dioxide is heavier than air when they are at the same temperature and pressure, but when carbon dioxide is produced by combustion, its temperature is higher than that of air. So carbon dioxide becomes lighter than air at that time. Because with increasing temperature, the density of any gas decreases so lighter air replaces air near the roof and can be easily detected.

Hence, the correct option is (B).

80. Hydrogen can be detected with a multi-gas detector or by chemical analysis. Hydrogen gas detection at different utilization stages is essential due to the explosive nature of the gas. Above 4% concentration level of hydrogen is highly explosive and dangerous. The small size of the H2 gas molecule leaks through small holes very easily.

Hence, the correct option is (B).

81. Manila rope is very durable, flexible, and resistant to saltwater damage, allowing its use in rope, hawsers, ships' lines, and fishing nets. It can be used to make handcrafts like bags, carpets, clothing, furniture, and hangings. Manila ropes shrink when they become wet.

Hence, the correct option is (A).

82. A forklift is a small industrial vehicle, having a power operated forked platform attached at the front that can be raised and lowered for insertion under a cargo to lift or move it. Forklifts are powered by electric batteries or combustion engines.

Hence, the correct option is (C).

83. Wheelbarrows are used for a variety of things, such as moving rock, mulch, or compost to the garden, moving trees or large shrubs from one spot to another, hauling bricks, disposing of garden debris, or even for mixing concrete or fertilizers.

Hence, the correct option is (A).

84. A crane is a major type of construction machine that is used to move the loads horizontally. Equipped with a hoist rope, wire ropes, and sheaves, it can be used to lift heavy loads or transport them to other places. The mechanical advantages created by several components on the crane can produce powerful strength.

Hence, the correct option is (C).

85. The pumps are classified on the basis of the principle of mechanical operation, type of power, and type of service.

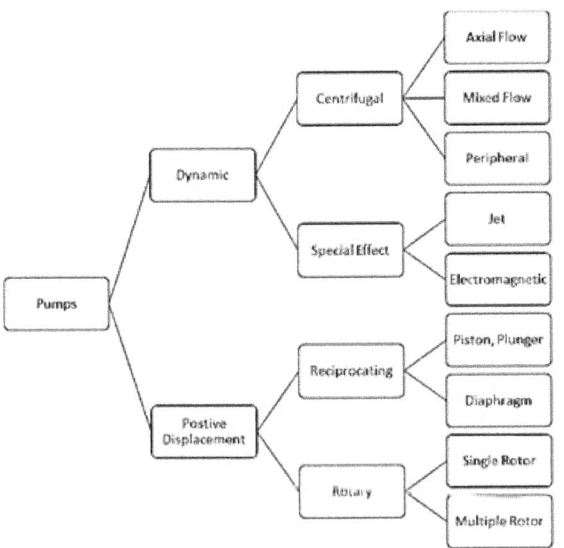

Hence, the correct option is (B).

86. According to the principle of Mechanical operation displacement pump is classified into centrifugal, airlift, and miscellaneous pumps.

A displacement pump moves a fluid by repeatedly enclosing a fixed volume, with the aid of seals or valves, and moving it mechanically through the system. The pumping action is cyclic and can be driven by pistons, screws, gears, lobes, diaphragms, or vanes.

Hence, the correct option is (A).

87. Sectionalizing means installing more number of small units rather than installing a big unit. Doing so enables us to maintain continuity of supply from the rest of the units when one or two units of plant fail. This makes the plant more reliable.

Hence, the correct option is (A).

88. The ratio of area under the curve to the total area of the rectangle is called the load factor.

The ratio of area under the curve to the number of hours represents the average load.

The peak of the curve represents the maximum demand.

Hence, the correct option is (C).

89. Fujairah Free Zone (FFZ) is a special economic zone in Fujairah, which is one of the seven emirates that comprise the United Arab Emirates. Fujairah Free Zone is located just north of the emirate's capital, Fujairah City. It is run by the Fujairah Free Zone Authority (FFZA).

Free-trade zone, also called foreign-trade zone, formerly free port, an area within which goods may be landed, handled, manufactured or reconfigured, and reexported without the intervention of the customs authorities.

Hence, the correct option is (A).

90. Direct payments made by the government to domestic companies to encourage exports or to protect them from imports are known as subsidies.

Subsidies are provided by the government to specific industries with the aim of keeping the prices of products and services low for people to be able to afford them and also to encourage production and consumption.

Hence, the correct option is (B).

91. The load curve is obtained by plotting fluctuating load by keeping the load on the y-axis and time on the x-axis.

The area under the load curve represents the total number of units generated at a particular time.

Hence, the correct option is (C).

92. Fuse is the current interrupting device that breaks or opens the circuit (in which it is inserted) by fusing the elements when the current in the circuit exceeds a certain value.

Hence, the correct option is (C).

93. The routine tests are performed on each individual circuit breaker of a proven design. The purpose is to prove the correctness of the assembly and the material used and to check the proper functioning of the circuit breaker.

Hence, the correct option is (D).

94. A Silicon-controlled rectifier or semiconductor-controlled rectifier is a four-layer solid-state current-controlling unidirectional device (i.e. can conduct current only in one direction).

The thyristor or silicon controlled rectifier is a three-terminal device labeled: "Anode", "Cathode" and "Gate" and consisting of three PN junctions that can be Switched "ON" and "OFF" at an extremely fast rate. or it can be switched "ON" for variable lengths of time during half cycles to deliver a selected amount of power to a load.

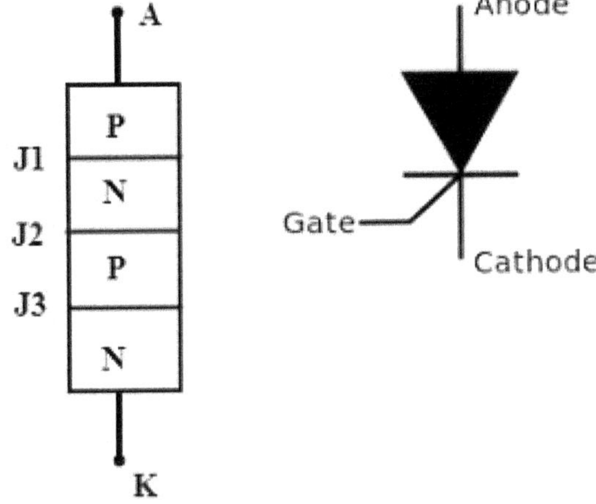

Hence, the correct option is (B).

95. The thyristor is also called a silicon-controlled rectifier (SCR), is basically a four-layer three-junction PNPN device. It has three terminals: anode, cathode, and gate. It is basically an electronic switching device that can remain in a conducting (on) and nonconducting state. However, it is a unidirectional device and can conduct only in one direction like a diode. The switching state of the device can be controlled by one of its terminals.

Hence, the correct option is (A).

96. Surveying is the art and science of determining the relative position of points on, above, or beneath the surface of the earth by means of direct or indirect measurement of distance direction or elevation. The Application of Surveying required skills as well as the knowledge of mathematics, physics, and to some extent astronomy.

Hence, the correct option is (A).

97. Levelling is a process of determining the height of one level relative to another. It is used in surveying to establish the elevation of a point relative to a datum or to establish a point at a given elevation relative to a datum.

Hence, the correct option is (A).

98. A normal equation is formed by the multiplication of unknown coefficients by which, the obtained equation is added and leads to the formation of a normal equation. If the number of equations formed is equal to the number of unknowns then the most probable values can be found by the equations.

Hence, the correct option is (A).

99. The correlates are also known as the unknown multiples, which are used for finding the most probable values of unknowns. It is more preferable when the case is more complex to be solved.

Hence, the correct option is (A).

100. The method of correlates is used in case of more complexity. In that case, it involves the usage of all the information available and the conditions mentioned so that it provides the result regarding the problem raised.

Hence, the correct option is (C).

Mock Test 03

General knowledge And Current Affairs

Q.1 Who among the following cricketers has won the ESPNcricinfo 'Captain of the Year' awards 2022?

A. Kane Williamson **B.** KL Rahul
C. Virat Kohli **D.** Babar Azam

Q.2 The treaty of Srirangapatna was signed between Tipu Sultan and:

A. Robert Clive **B.** Cornwallis
C. Dalhousie **D.** Warren Hastings

Q.3 The only private sector refinery set up by Reliance Petroleum Ltd. is located at:

A. Guwahati **B.** Jamnagar
C. Mumbai **D.** Chennai

Q.4 Which state government has proposed to set-up its 6th Ramona National Park?

A. Assam **B.** Madhya Pradesh
C. Bihar **D.** Paschim Bengal

Q.5 NASA-ISRO is to launch NISAR satellite in which year?

A. 2020 **B.** 2021 **C.** 2022 **D.** 2025

Q.6 The National Skill Development Corporation, a not-for-profit public limited company has joined hands with which company to enhance the digital skills of the country's youth?

A. Paytm **B.** Facebook
C. Google **D.** Microsoft

Q.7 Mahdi Mohammed Gulaid is appointed as interim Prime Minister of which country?

A. Slovakia **B.** Slovenia **C.** Somalia **D.** Croatia

Q.8 The objective of the Morley-Minto Reforms was:

A. Extension of provincial assemblies
B. To give more powers to local government
C. To abolish the post of secretary of the state for India
D. To establish diarchy in provinces

Q.9 In which decade did the first transatlantic radio broadcast occur?

A. 1850s **B.** 1860s **C.** 1870s **D.** 1900s

Q.10 Redistribution policies geared to reduce economic inequalities include:

A. Progressive tax policies
B. Land reforms
C. Rural development policies
D. All the above

Mine management, Legislation and General Safety

Q.11 The term "Learning Organisation" means:

A. People of all levels, individually or collectively are continually increasing their capacity to produce results, they care about
B. A collective ideal, a vision
C. It promotes the culture of Learning, a community of learners, and it ensures that individual learning enriches & enhances the organization as a whole
D. All of the above

Q.12 Line Management is:

A. Hierarchical chain of command from executive to front-line level in which top management has direct authority
B. Organized along cross-functional lines, such as employee development or strategic direction
C. Both (A) and (B)
D. None of the above

Q.13 ____ is a process of transmission of massage and understanding of information between two or more people, it involves at least two parties-a senders and a receiver.

A. Body language **B.** Communication
C. System **D.** None of the above

Q.14 ________ methods are generally applied to the workplace while employees are actually working.

A. On-the-job training **B.** Off-the-job training
C. Both (A) and (B) **D.** None of the above

Q.15 "____________ are social inventions for accomplishing goals through group efforts".

A. Management **B.** Organization
C. Leadership **D.** Behaviour

Q.16 Neo-classical Theory of Organisation consists.

A. Decentralisation
B. Non-formal Organisation
C. Human-oriented
D. All of the above

Q.17 Which of the following is/are not the job-related source of stress?

A. Role ambiguity **B.** Role overload
C. Ethical dilemmas **D.** Career concerns

Q.18 A graphical device used to determine the break-even point and profit potential under varying conditions of output and costs, is known as:

A. Gnatt chart **B.** Flow chart
C. Break-even chart **D.** PERT chart

Q.19 Break-even analysis consists of:

A. Fixed cost
B. Variable cost
C. Fixed and variable costs
D. Operation costs

Q.20 Break-even analysis shows profit when:
A. Sales revenue > total cost
B. Sales revenue = total cost
C. Sales revenue < total cos
D. Variable cost < fixed cost

Q.21 What does the symbol 'D' imply in work-study?
A. Inspection
B. Transport
C. Delay temporary storage
D. Permanent storage

Q.22 Financial leverage measures_______.
A. The sensitivity of EBIT with respect to % change with respect to output
B. % variation in the level of production
C. The sensitivity of EPS with respect to % change in the level of EBIT
D. No change with EBIT and EPS

Q.23 "Quality is defined by the customer" is:
A. An unrealistic definition of quality
B. A user-based definition of quality
C. A manufacturing-based definition of quality
D. A product-based definition of quality

Q.24 According to the manufacturing-based definition of quality:
A. Quality is the degree of excellence at an acceptable price and the control of variability at an acceptable cost
B. Quality depends on how well the product fits patterns of consumer preferences even though
C. Quality cannot be defined, you know what it is
D. Quality is the degree to which a specific product conforms to standards

Q.25 The supply chain concept originated in what discipline?
A. Marketing B. Operations
C. Logistics D. Production

Q.26 In a network, a critical path is the time-wise:
A. Longest path B. Shortest path
C. Normal path D. None of the above

Q.27 The difference between the maximum time available and the actual time needed to perform an activity is known as _______.
A. Free float B. Independent float
C. Total float D. Half float

Q.28 Which of the following types of personality is comparatively less exposed to internal stress?
A. Type A personality B. Type B personality
C. Type C personality D. None of the above

Q.29 The term for the workmen inspector is:
A. 5 years B. 3 years C. 2 years D. 6 years

Q.30 The owner, manager or agent shall take action on the report of the workmen's inspector within a period of______from the date of entry into the register.
A. 7 days B. 30 days C. 15 days D. 10 days

Q.31 The owner, agent or manager shall constitute a 'safety committee' for promoting safety in the mine for more than ....persons are ordinarily employed in every mine.
A. 500 B. 1000 C. 50 D. 100

Q.32 The number of members is nominated for the safety committee is:
A. 5 B. 10 C. 13 D. 15

Q.33 The owner, agent or manager shall within a period from the date of receipt of the recommendations of the safety committee indicate to the secretary to the safety committee, the action taken to implement the recommendations:
A. 7 days B. 30 days C. 15 days D. 10 days

Q.34 What does section 44 refer to?
A. Penalty for interference with meters
B. Penalty for illegal transmission or use of energy
C. Penalty for maliciously wasting energy
D. Theft of energy

Q.35 The safety committee shall meet at least once in:
A. 15 days B. 7 days
C. 6 months D. 3 months

Q.36 Which section in the IE Act deals with the 'theft of energy'?
A. Section 39 B. Section 40
C. Section 43 D. Section 44

Q.37 Which rule deals with the supply to X- rays and high-frequency installations?
A. Rule 30 B. Rule 39 C. Rule 73 D. Rule 51

Q.38 What is meant by petty purchase?
A. An item purchased from the market by purchase assistant with proper formal order
B. An item purchased from the market by purchase assistant with proper formal order
C. A single tendering purchase
D. None of these

Q.39 The __________ process determines whether exposure to a chemical can increase the incidence of adverse health effect.
A. Hazard identification
B. Exposure assessment
C. Toxicity assessment
D. Risk characterization

Q.40 Which of the following data is not required for hazard identification?
A. Land use B. Contaminant levels
C. Affected population D. Estimation of risk

Winning and Working

Q.41 What is the cleavage shown by quartz minerals?
A. Basal **B.** Prismatic
C. Rhombohedral **D.** No cleavage

Q.42 Quartz is found in which type of rock?
A. Igneous rock
B. Sedimentary rock
C. Metamorphic rock
D. Igneous, sedimentary and metamorphic rocks

Q.43 Low-grade brown coal is called:
A. Magnetite **B.** Bauxite
C. Lignite **D.** Limonite

Q.44 The core (diameter in mm) size obtained with NX size?
A. 21 **B.** 28 **C.** 40 **D.** 54

Q.45 Manual drilling is possible up to the max depth of ____ m.
A. 15 **B.** 25 **C.** 45 **D.** 60

Q.46 Which central government agency is responsible for the mapping and exploration of minerals?
A. The Geological Survey of India
B. Surveyor General of India
C. National Mineral Development Corporation Ltd
D. Indian Bureau of Mines

Q.47 The single tube core barrel is suitable for recovering core from rocks of:
A. Soft **B.** Friable
C. Homogeneous **D.** Hard

Q.48 The double tube core barrel is suitable for rocks of:
A. Hard **B.** Homogeneous
C. Soft and friable **D.** None of the above

Q.49 Under which rule of the Mines Rule, 1955 constitution of a statutory safety committee has been made mandatory where 100 workers are generally employed in a mine?
A. Rule 28(T) **B.** Rule 36(T)
C. Rule 29(T) **D.** Rule 49(T)

Q.50 In which of the following milling machine, the table can be tilted in a vertical plane by providing a swivel arrangement at the knee?
A. Horizontal milling machine
B. Plain milling machine
C. Universal milling machine
D. Hand milling machine

Q.51 A 15 mm drilling machine means that it can drill a hole:
A. Of maximum diameter 15 mm
B. In 15 mm thick plates
C. Having a cross-sectional area of 15 mm^2
D. None of these

Q.52 The tool life is said to be over if:
A. Poor surface finish is obtained
B. There is a sudden increase in cutting forces and power consumption
C. Overheating and fuming due to heat of friction starts
D. All of the above

Q.53 A fixture is defined as a device which:
A. Holds and locates a workpiece and guides and controls one or more cutting tools
B. Holds and locates a workpiece during an inspection or for a manufacturing operation
C. Is used to check the accuracy of the workpiece
D. All of the above

Q.54 High-speed steel drills can be operated at about ________ the speed of high carbon steel drills.
A. One-half **B.** One-fourth
C. Double **D.** Four times

Q.55 At least how much % of the packed explosives are less effective than bulk explosives?
A. 10 **B.** 15 **C.** 20 **D.** 25

Q.56 Deadtime of the instrument is:
A. The time required by an instrument to begin to respond to a change in the measurand
B. The time required by an instrument for initial warming up
C. The largest change of input quantity for which there is no output of the instrument
D. None of the above

Q.57 In electrical measuring instruments electrical energy is converted to:
A. Mechanical energy **B.** Heat energy
C. Chemical energy **D.** Light energy

Q.58 Torque weight ratio will be least in .... instruments.
A. Dynamometer **B.** Moving iron
C. Moving coil **D.** All of the above

Q.59 Vibrating reeds are used in which of the following instruments:
A. Power factor meter
B. Frequency factor meter
C. Wattmeter
D. Synchronoscope

Q.60 Scale of an instrument will be uniform if:
A. Deflecting torque varies directly as the deflection angle
B. Control torque varies directly as the deflection angle
C. Both (A) and (B)
D. Damping torque varies directly as the deflection angle

Surface environment, Mine Ventilation and Hazards

Q.61 What specific aspects do a good EIA report and review include?
1. Assessment, mitigation measures and related plans.

2. A terms of reference (TOR).
3. A generalized set of assumptions about the project benefits described in highly technical terms.
4. A satisfactory prediction of the adverse effects of proposed actions and their mitigation using conventional and customized techniques.
5. Information that is helpful and relevant to decision making.

A. 2,3,4 **B.** 1,2,4,5
C. 1,2,3,4,5 **D.** None of the above

Q.62 Depending on the EIA system, responsibility for producing an EIA will be assigned:
A. The government agency or ministry
B. The project proponent
C. Both (A) and (B)
D. None of the above

Q.63 ________ is a process which involves further removal of the nitrogen.
A. Nitrification **B.** Denitrification
C. Ammonification **D.** Reduction

Q.64 In rotating biological contractors, what percent of corrugated plastic discs are submerged?
A. 20 **B.** 50 **C.** 80 **D.** 40

Q.65 The rank of India in terms of water availability per person per annum in the world is____________.
A. 130th **B.** 131st **C.** 132nd **D.** 133rd

Q.66 Ground water is accessed by___________.
A. Drilling wells **B.** Drip irrigation
C. Check bunds **D.** Constructing canals

Q.67 Which of the following is not a desirable feature of the ovens used in gas chromatography?
A. It must have a fast rate of heating
B. Power consumption should be kept low
C. It must have maximum thermal gradients
D. It should have proper insulation

Q.68 Given below is the block diagram of gas chromatography. Identify the unmarked component.

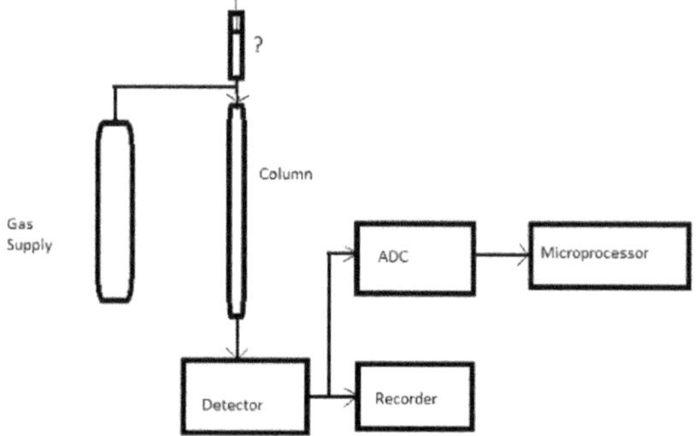

A. Pumping system
B. Pressure regulator
C. Flow regulator
D. Sample injection system

Q.69 The ratio between H.P of ventilation and H.P. of the fan shaft is called:
A. Mechanical efficiency
B. Manometric efficiency
C. Overall efficiency
D. None of these

Q.70 The ratio between H.P of ventilation and H.P input to the engine is called:
A. Mechanical efficiency
B. Manometric efficiency
C. Overall efficiency
D. Fan efficiency

Q.71 What would be the amount of distance that a low-pressure system could carry the ash?
A. 25m **B.** 500m **C.** 150m **D.** 800m

Q.72 What is the capacity of the low-pressure hydraulic ash handling system?
A. 80 tonnes/hour **B.** 22 tonnes/hour
C. 50 tonnes/hour **D.** 10 tonnes/hour

Q.73 Which one of the following is another name of RDX?
A. Cyanohydrin **B.** Dextran
C. Cyclohexane **D.** Cyclonite

Q.74 Which one of the following is also called stranger gas?
A. Argon **B.** Neon
C. Xenon **D.** Nitrous oxide

Q.75 ___________ is a non-combustible building material, but it is a good conductor of heat and hence, it is rapidly heated in case of a fire.
A. Glass **B.** Brick
C. Limestone **D.** Steel

Q.76 _____________ is a very good conductor of heat.
A. Asbestos cement **B.** Aluminium
C. Cast iron **D.** Wrought iron

Q.77 A land is said to be water-logged when ___________
A. The aeration is stopped in the root zone due to the rise in water content
B. There is a reduction in crop yield
C. There is an accumulation of alkali salts in the root zone of the crop
D. There is salinity in the soil

Q.78 What is the pH range for strongly alkaline soils?
A. 7.4 – 7.8 **B.** 7.9 – 8.4 **C.** 8.5 – 9.0 **D.** > 9

Q.79 Presence of excessive moisture _______the bacterial activities affecting crop growth.
A. Retards **B.** Increase
C. Kill **D.** None of these

Q.80 Which of the following statement is wrong?
A. Seepage drains reduce the chances of water-logging

B. Untimely maturity of the crops is the characteristic of water-logged lands
C. The percolation loss can be reduced by keeping the intensity of irrigation low
D. There is no way to keep a watch over the problem of Water-logging

Mine Machineries, surveying and electricity

Q.81 Which of the following slings is best to use when flexibility, high strength, and resistance to rotation are essential?
A. Braided slings **B.** Cable-laid slings
C. Fibre rope slings **D.** Strand-laid slings

Q.82 Which of the following is true of alloy steel chains?
A. They should not be used in situations where the failure of the chain would result in serious property damage
B. They are suitable for high-temperature operations
C. They should never be used for slings
D. Their tensile strength decreases in proportion to their hardness

Q.83 Steel wire ropes are specified by:
A. Weight of the wire per meter length
B. Nominal rope diameter in millimeters followed by the number of strands and the number of wires in a strand
C. Breaking load in kN followed by diameter of the strand in millimeters and number of wires in a strand
D. None of these

Q.84 An essential requirement of a good MH system is:
A. Capital cost expenditure
B. Flexibility reduction
C. Saleability of plant & equipment
D. Storing materials utilizing minimum space

Q.85 The motor in close is used for collieries, the chemical plant is:
A. Flameproof type
B. Splash-proof type
C. Totally enclosed type
D. Pipe ventilated type

Q.86 The motor enclosure used in the wood-working industry is:
A. Protected type
B. Totally Enclosed Fan-Cooled type
C. Flameproof type
D. Splash-proof type

Q.87 The motor enclosure used for industrial purposes is:
A. Protected type
B. Drip-proof type
C. Totally enclosed type
D. Open type

Q.88 The Regression coefficient is independent of:
A. Origin
B. Scale
C. Both origin and scale
D. Neither origin nor scale

Q.89 Ample conditions were used in the method of :
A. Linear equation **B.** Correlation
C. Quadratic equation **D.** None of these

Q.90 Which of the following does not indicate the feature in-laws of accidental errors?
A. Negligible errors **B.** Small errors
C. Large errors **D.** Positive errors

Q.91 Most probable value is equal to which of the following?
A. Differentiation **B.** Summation
C. Arithmetic mean **D.** Normal equation

Q.92 Which of the following represents SI unit of luminous intensity?
A. Candela **B.** Lumen
C. Dioptre **D.** None of the above

Q.93 Probability curve describes about____________.
A. Normal equation **B.** Frequency of errors
C. Logistic regression **D.** Probability equation

Q.94 The basic difference between MRP-I and MRP-II is:
A. Inventory **B.** Bom
C. Finance **D.** Capacity planning

Q.95 Inventory record file gives the following information:
A. Lot size **B.** Machine details
C. Customer name **D.** None of the above

Q.96 Which of the following features should be shown in the water safety plan?
A. Position of dyke, fault and geological disturbances
B. River, stream, watercourse, reservoir
C. Surface contour lines
D. All of the above

Q.97 Which of the following is not used in the tracking system?
A. Multiple frequency **B.** Dual-frequency
C. Single-frequency **D.** Military navigation

Q.98 Which of the following doesn't belong to the relative positioning techniques?
A. Real-time kinematic technique
B. Viscous GPS technique
C. Kinematic GPS surveying technique
D. Differential GPS technique

Q.99 Which of the following classes of positioning technique possess high precision?
A. GPS
B. Viscous technique
C. Real-time technique
D. Kinematic technique

Q.100 Which of the following is considered as modern GPS technology?

A. GIS
B. GPS mode
C. Instantaneous mode
D. Kinematic positioning technique

// Smart Answer Sheet //

Correct: Percentage of students who answered correctly. Skipped: Percentage of students who skipped.

Q.	Ans.	Correct	Skipped	Q.	Ans.	Correct	Skipped	Q.	Ans.	Correct	Skipped	Q.	Ans.	Correct	Skipped	Q.	Ans.	Correct	Skipped	Q.	Ans.	Correct	Skipped
1	C	89.77 %	0.0 %	18	C	49.05 %	1.73 %	35	D	60.14 %	1.63 %	52	D	78.77 %	0.0 %	69	D	44.39 %	1.41 %	86	B	68.54 %	1.19 %
2	B	59.26 %	1.69 %	19	C	46.48 %	1.71 %	36	A	56.02 %	1.33 %	53	B	55.25 %	1.68 %	70	A	57.29 %	1.7 %	87	A	78.41 %	0.0 %
3	B	80.05 %	0.0 %	20	A	13.46 %	4.01 %	37	C	68.13 %	1.95 %	54	C	60.04 %	1.75 %	71	B	24.06 %	4.67 %	88	A	45.93 %	1.76 %
4	A	64.6 %	1.65 %	21	C	82.02 %	0.0 %	38	B	81.16 %	0.0 %	55	B	41.41 %	1.55 %	72	C	58.81 %	1.3 %	89	B	68.17 %	1.16 %
5	C	69.07 %	1.16 %	22	C	76.92 %	0.0 %	39	A	42.86 %	1.23 %	56	B	56.99 %	1.93 %	73	D	85.01 %	0.0 %	90	A	88.65 %	0.0 %
6	D	53.64 %	1.63 %	23	B	57.32 %	2.0 %	40	D	56.98 %	1.64 %	57	A	80.43 %	0.0 %	74	C	61.9 %	1.48 %	91	C	40.75 %	1.29 %
7	C	82.95 %	0.0 %	24	D	82.44 %	0.0 %	41	D	80.05 %	0.0 %	58	A	53.45 %	1.77 %	75	D	57.56 %	1.77 %	92	A	63.26 %	1.24 %
8	A	21.69 %	3.77 %	25	A	57.06 %	1.48 %	42	D	68.81 %	1.96 %	59	B	57.15 %	1.17 %	76	B	76.07 %	0.0 %	93	B	26.87 %	3.01 %
9	D	84.6 %	0.0 %	26	A	59.29 %	1.23 %	43	C	40.1 %	1.16 %	60	C	48.05 %	1.62 %	77	A	64.76 %	1.06 %	94	C	69.07 %	1.91 %
10	D	66.32 %	1.93 %	27	C	61.96 %	1.98 %	44	D	47.84 %	1.94 %	61	B	30.63 %	3.62 %	78	C	58.75 %	1.98 %	95	A	77.05 %	0.0 %
11	D	50.59 %	1.9 %	28	B	57.63 %	1.14 %	45	B	76.1 %	0.0 %	62	C	67.99 %	1.75 %	79	A	52.79 %	1.52 %	96	D	81.79 %	0.0 %
12	C	82.37 %	0.0 %	29	B	84.71 %	0.0 %	46	A	53.61 %	1.28 %	63	B	31.69 %	4.22 %	80	D	40.77 %	1.6 %	97	A	88.91 %	0.0 %
13	B	67.02 %	1.25 %	30	C	44.57 %	1.14 %	47	C	68.21 %	1.32 %	64	D	52.51 %	1.04 %	81	A	40.56 %	1.3 %	98	B	62.84 %	1.59 %
14	A	76.37 %	0.0 %	31	D	27.81 %	3.95 %	48	C	79.62 %	0.0 %	65	D	78.54 %	0.0 %	82	B	54.68 %	1.5 %	99	D	62.83 %	1.93 %
15	B	57.39 %	1.31 %	32	C	84.93 %	0.0 %	49	C	52.66 %	1.8 %	66	A	66.76 %	1.47 %	83	B	63.78 %	1.84 %	100	D	55.34 %	1.31 %
16	D	28.09 %	4.78 %	33	C	56.8 %	1.53 %	50	C	44.83 %	1.34 %	67	C	14.9 %	4.04 %	84	D	55.0 %	1.24 %				
17	D	85.46 %	0.0 %	34	A	50.52 %	1.3 %	51	A	81.41 %	0.0 %	68	D	83.41 %	0.0 %	85	A	64.63 %	1.09 %				

//Hints and Solutions//

1. New Zealand skipper Kane Williamson was adjudged 'Captain of the Year' at the 15th Annual ESPNcricinfo awards 2022.

Williamson won it for leading his side to the World Test Championship win and a runners-up place at the T20 World Cup. The jury picked the best performances in the three men's international formats, and performances in women's cricket at large, in the 2021 calendar year.

Hence, the correct option is (C).

2. The Treaty of Seringapatam (also called Srirangapatinam or Srirangapatna), signed on 18th March 1792, ended the Third Anglo-Mysore War. Its signatories included Lord Cornwallis on behalf of the British East India Company, representatives of the Nizam of Hyderabad and the Maratha Empire, and Tipu Sultan, the ruler of Mysore.

Hence, the correct option is (B).

3. Jamnagar is known as 'World's Oil City' because the world's biggest oil refineries, belonging to Reliance Industries and Nayara Energy, are here. Reliance Industries refinery: The Jamnagar Refinery is a private sector crude oil refinery owned by Reliance Industries Limited.

Hence, the correct option is (B).

4. The Assam government has proposed to set-up a 6th national park in a militancy ravaged reserve forest.

Assam Chief Minister Sarbananda Sonowal on July 6, 2020, announced that the government has decided that Dehing Patkai Wildlife Sanctuary will soon be upgraded into National Park. At present, Assam has five national parks—Kaziranga National Park, Manas National Park, Nameri National Park, Dibru-Saikhowa National Park and Orang National Park. Dima Hasao district will soon get its first and the state's sixth national park. Dima Hasao is one of the least explored pockets of Assam even though it is home to the state's one and only hill station Haflong and is the greenest district in the entire state.

Hence, the correct option is (A).

5. India and the US recently held the two plus two dialogue. During the meet the country's decision to share space situational awareness information. This will catalyse efforts in creating safe and sustainable space environment A joint statement issued after the dialogue read that the NASA-ISRO Synthetic Aperture Radar called the NISAR is to be launched by 2022.

Hence, the correct option is (C).

6. The National Skill Development Corporation (NSDC), a not-for-profit public limited company has joined hands with tech giant company Microsoft India Private Limited, a subsidiary of American software company Microsoft Corporation, to enhance the digital skills of the country's youth. Under this, more than 1 lakh youth will be digitally enabled in the country in the next one year.

Hence, the correct option is (D).

7. President of Somalia, Mohamed Abdullahi Mohamed appointed Deputy Prime Minister Mahdi Mohammed Gulaid as the interim Prime Minister of Somalia following the impeachment of Hassan Ali Khaire, the previous Prime Minister of Somalia.

Hence, the correct option is (C).

8. Morley-Minto Reforms of 1909 was primarily aimed at extending Provincial Assemblies. The reforms established Indian dominance in the provincial, but not central, legislative bodies. Elections, mainly indirect, were affirmed for all levels of society. The elected Indians were also enabled to debate budgetary and complementary matters and table resolutions.

Hence, the correct option is (A).

9. In the 1900s decade, the first transatlantic radio broadcast occurred.

On December 12, 1901, a radio transmission received by Guglielmo Marconi resulted in the first transmission of a transatlantic wireless signal (Morse Code) from Poldhu, Cornwall, to St. John's, Newfoundland. The signals had traveled a distance of 3500 kilometers.

Hence, the correct option is (D).

10. Redistribution policies geared to reduce economic inequalities include progressive tax policies, land reforms and rural development policies.

Redistribution of income and wealth is the transfer of income and wealth (including physical property) from some individuals to others by means of a social mechanism such as taxation, charity, welfare, public services, land reform, monetary policies, confiscation, divorce or tort law.

Hence, the correct option is (D).

11. A learning organization is an organization skilled at creating, acquiring, and transferring knowledge, and at modifying its behavior to reflect new knowledge and insights. Whatever their source, these ideas are the trigger for organizational improvement. But they cannot by themselves create a learning organization.

Hence, the correct option is (D).

12. Line management refers to the management of employees who are directly involved in the production or delivery of products, goods, and/or services. As the interface between an organization and its front-line workforce, line management represents the lowest level of management within an organizational hierarchy (as distinct from top/executive/senior management and middle management).

Hence, the correct option is (C).

13. Communication is a process of transmission of massage and understanding of information between two or more people, it involves at least two parties-a senders and a receiver. The transmission of the message from sender to recipient can be affected by a huge range of things. These include our emotions, the cultural situation, the medium used to communicate, and even our location. The complexity is why good communication skills are considered so desirable by employers around the world:

accurate, effective and unambiguous communication is actually extremely hard.

Hence, the correct option is (B).

14. On-the-job training methods are generally applied to the workplace while employees are actually working.

On-the-job Training (OJT) means training in the public or private sector that is given to a paid employee while he or she is engaged in productive work and that provides knowledge and skills essential to the full and adequate performance on the job.

Hence, the correct option is (A).

15. "Organisations are social inventions for accomplishing goals through group efforts".

An organization is a group of people who work together, like a neighbourhood association, a charity, a union, or a corporation. The organization is also the act of forming or establishing something (like an organization). It can also refer to a system of arrangement or order or a structure for classifying things.

Hence, the correct option is (B).

16. The neoclassical theory was an attempt at incorporating the behavioral sciences into management thought in order to solve the problems caused by classical theory practices. The premise of this inclusion was based on the idea that the role of management is to use employees to get things done in organizations.

Hence, the correct option is (D).

17. A career means you stay in the same type of work. A career can be one job or many jobs. A career is sometimes called a "career path." A career includes education, training, and work experience. In a career, you need to think about how you can grow in your job or move into another job.

Role ambiguity, role overload and ethical dilemmas are job-related sources of stress.

Hence, the correct option is (D).

18. A graphical device used to determine the break-even point and profit potential under varying conditions of output and costs is known as a break-even chart.

The break-even point can be calculated by drawing a graph showing how fixed costs, variable costs, total costs and total revenue change with the level of output.

Hence, the correct option is (C).

19. Break-even analysis consists of fixed and variable costs.

Fixed costs are expenses that remain constant for a period of time irrespective of the level of outputs. Variable costs are expenses that change directly and proportionally to the changes in business activity level or volume.

Hence, the correct option is (C).

20. Break-even analysis shows profit when sales revenue ">" total cost.

Break-Even Analysis in economics, business, and cost accounting refers to the point in which total cost and total revenue are equal.

A break-even point analysis is used to determine the number of units or dollars of revenue needed to cover total costs (fixed and variable costs).

The formula for break-even analysis is as follows:

Break-even quantity = Fixed costs / (Sales price per unit – Variable cost per unit).

Where:

- Fixed costs are costs that do not change with varying output (e.g., salary, rent, building machinery).
- Sales price per unit is the selling price (unit selling price) per unit.
- Variable cost per unit is the variable costs incurred to create a unit.

Hence, the correct option is (A).

21. A delay occurs when the immediate performance of the next planned thing does not take place. Example: Work waiting between consecutive operations. This also leads into temporary storage.

Hence, the correct option is (A).

22. The Financial Leverage (FL) measures the relationship between the EBIT (Earnings Before Interest and Taxes) and the EPS (Earning Per Share) and it reflects the effect of change in EBIT on the level of EPS. The FL measures the responsiveness of the EPS to a change in EBIT and is defined as the % change in EPS divided by the % change in EBIT.

Hence, the correct option is (C).

23. Quality is an ever-evolving perception by the customer of the value provided by a product. The customer's definition of Quality is the only one that counts. The totality of features and characteristics of a product or service that bears on its ability to satisfy given needs. Quality is not achieved by doing different things. It is achieved by doing things differently.

Hence, the correct option is (B).

24. According to the manufacturing-based definition of quality is the degree to which a specific product conforms to standards. manufacturing-based definitions focus on the supply side of the equation and are primarily concerned with engineering and manufacturing practice. Virtually all manufacturing-based definitions identify quality as "conformance to requirements."

Hence, the correct option is (D).

25. The marketing supply chain is the chain of suppliers that an organization relies on to produce marketing materials (print, promotional products and point of sale) to market their products and services. The marketing supply chain is often made up of partners inside and outside of the organization – such as brand managers, marketing services, agencies, direct sales teams, buyers, printers, fulfillment houses and many others.

Hence, the correct option is (A).

26. In a network, a critical path is the time-wise longest path. The critical path in the Critical Path Method plays an essential role in scheduling and planning. In project management, a critical path is the sequence of project network activities that add up to the longest overall duration, regardless if that longest duration has float or not. This determines the shortest time possible to complete the project.

Hence, the correct option is (A).

27. The difference between the maximum time available and the actual time needed to perform an activity is known as the total float. Hence, the total float is the excess of the maximum available time throughout the time of the activity.

Hence, the correct option is (C).

28. Type B personality is considered the healthiest and the most common. People with this personality type are flexible and docile. They're calm, relaxed, empathetic, assertive, open to social relationships, and have a tendency toward emotional well-being. In general, they're aware of their limitations and aren't hostile.

Hence, the correct option is (B).

29. A Workmen's Inspector nominated under sub-rule(1) shall, unless he resigns from his office, hold office for a period of three years from the date of his nomination and shall be eligible for one renomination.

When the number of persons employed in a mine exceeds 1500, the workmen's inspector shall be assisted by one additional workmen's inspector in the mining discipline for every additional 1000 persons.

Hence, the correct option is (B).

30. The owner, agent or manager of the mine shall enter in the register mentioned in sub-rule (2) of rule 29R, within a period of 15 days from the date of entry in the register, remarks thereon showing the remedial measures are taken and the date on which such action was taken.

Hence, the correct option is (C).

31. Safety Committee - For every mine wherein more than 100 persons are ordinarily employed, the owner, agent or manager shall constitute a safety committee for promoting safety in the mine.

Hence, the correct option is (D).

32. The number of members is nominated for the safety committee is 13.

Composition of Safety Committee - The safety committee shall consist of -

(a) The manager who shall be the Chairman,

(b) Five officials or competent persons of the mine nominated by the Chairman,

(c) Five workmen nominated by the workmen of the mine accordance with the procedure prescribed in clause (a) of sub-rule(1) of rule 29Q for the nomination of workmen's inspector,

(d) Workmen's Inspector, and

(e) the Safety Officer, or where there is no Safety Officer, senior-most mine Official next to the manager, who shall as Secretary to the Committee; Provided that any other official, competent person or workperson may be co-opted by the Chairman as a member of the committee on any day or days of the meeting. If considered necessary.

Hence, the correct option is (C).

33. 29W Implementation of recommendations of the Safety Committee - The owner, agent or manager shall, within a period of 15 days from the date of receipt of the recommendations of the Safety Committee, shall indicate to the Secretary to the Safety Committee, the action taken to implement the recommendations.

Hence, the correct option is (C).

34. Section 44 in The Indian Electricity Act, 1910 Penalty for interference with meters or licensee's works and for improper use of energy. Whoever improperly uses the energy of a licensee, shall be punishable with imprisonment for a term which may extend to three years, or with fine which may extend to five thousand rupees, or with both.

Hence, the correct option is (A).

35. The safety committee shall meet at least once in 3 months.

The safety committee shall meet at regular intervals at least once in every quarter, and minutes of the meetings shall be circulated to the concerned departments of the port, agencies and organizations.

Hence, the correct option is (D).

36. Section 39, in the IE Act, deals with the 'theft of energy'.

Whoever dishonestly abstracts, consumes or uses any energy shall be punishable with imprisonment for a term which may extend to three years, or with fine which shall not be less than one thousand rupees, or with both.

Hence, the correct option is (A).

37. Rule 73 deals with the supply to X-rays and high-frequency installations. According to this law, any person who proposes to employ or who is employing energy for the purpose of operating an X-ray or similar high-frequency installation, shall comply with the following conditions:

(a) Mechanical barriers shall be provided to prevent too close an approach to any high-voltage parts of the X-ray apparatus, except the X-ray tube and its leads unless such high-voltage parts have been rendered shock-proof by being shielded by earthed metal or adequate insulating material.

(b) Where extra-high voltage generators operating at 300 peak KV or more are used, such generators shall be installed in rooms separate from those containing the other equipment and any step-up transformer employed shall be so installed and protected as to prevent danger.

(c) A suitable switch shall be provided to control the circuit supplying a generator and shall be so arranged as to be open except while the door of the room housing the generator is locked from the outside.

(d) X-ray tubes used in therapy shall be mounted in an earthed metal enclosure.

(e) Every X-ray machine shall be provided with a millimeter or other suitable measuring instrument, readily visible from the control position and connected, if practicable, in the earthed lead, but guarded if connected in the high-voltage lead. 1[(ee) Notwithstanding the provisions of clause (e), the earth leakage circuit breaker of sufficient rating shall be provided on the low voltage side to detect the leakage in such X-ray installations].

(f) This sub-rule shall not apply to shock-proof portable units or shock-proof self-contained and stationary units.

Hence, the correct option is (C).

38. Petty purchase means, 'An item purchased from the market by purchase assistant with proper formal order'. Also, Petty cash is a small amount of cash that is kept on the company premises to pay for minor cash needs. Examples of these payments are office supplies, cards, flowers and so on.

Hence, the correct option Is (B).

39. The hazard identification process determines whether exposure to a chemical can increase the incidence of adverse health effects. Hazard identification is part of the process used to evaluate if any particular situation, item, thing, etc. may have the potential to cause harm. The term often used to describe the full process is risk assessment: Identify hazards and risk factors that have the potential to cause harm (hazard identification).

Hence, the correct option is (A).

40. Estimation of risk is not required for hazard identification.

Estimation of risk is done at risk characterization whereas land use, contaminant level, affected population and biota data play a major role while identifying a hazard.

Hence, the correct option is (D).

41. The cleavage is generally absent in the quartz minerals which is one of the defining characteristics of the quartz group. Quartz is a hard, crystalline mineral composed of silicon and oxygen atoms. it does not exhibit cleavage, although crystal faces may be mistaken for cleavage planes. Conchoidal fracture is characteristic of both macrocrystalline and cryptocrystalline quartz varieties.

Hence, the correct option is (D).

42. Quartz minerals are found in a wide range of rocks. They are not restricted to any one kind of rock. They may be found in igneous or sedimentary or metamorphic rocks. Quartz is the second most abundant mineral in Earth's crust after feldspar. It is an essential mineral in such silica-rich felsic rocks as granites, granodiorites, and rhyolites.

Hence, the correct option is (D).

43. Low-grade brown coal is called lignite. Lignite is often called "brown coal" because it is lighter in color than the higher ranks of coal. It has the lowest carbon content out of all the coal ranks (25%-35%)and it has high moisture content and crumbly texture.

Hence, the correct option is (C).

44. The borehole core recovery percentage incorporating only pieces of a solid core that is longer than 100 mm in length measured along the centerline of the core.

RQD was originally introduced for use with core diameters of 54.7 mm (NX-size core).

Hence, the correct option is (D).

45. Manual percussion drilling is generally used up to depths of 25 meters. Manual drilling refers to several drilling methods that rely on human energy to construct a borehole and complete a water supply. The various techniques can be used in areas where formations are quite soft and groundwater is relatively shallow. Manual drilling can provide safe drinking water.

Hence, the correct option is (B).

46. The Geological Survey of India agency is responsible for the mapping and exploration of minerals. Geological Survey of India [GSI], an attached office of the Ministry of Mines, proposes to take up aero geophysical survey of 8.13 lakh square kilometer of the geological potential area in the country through outsourcing.

Hence, the correct option is (A).

47. This core barrel is designed to obtain cores in homogenous formations. This core barrel does not have an inner tube and its utilization is justified when needing a lower per meter drilling cost than as with the double tube core barrel.

Hence, the correct option is (C).

48. The double tube core barret is suitable for rocks that are soft and friable.

The double tube core Barrels are swivel heads i.e the inner tube is attached with the core barrel head through bearings which makes the rotation of the inner tube independent of the core barrel. Water in the double tube core barrel passes in between the outer tube and inner tube.

Hence, the correct option is (C).

49. Under Section 29T in the Mines Rules, 1955 a safety committee is formed.

Safety Committee - For every mine wherein more than 100 persons are ordinarily employed, the owner, agent or manager shall constitute a Safety Committee for promoting Safety in the mine: Provided that the Chief Inspector or an Inspector may by a general or special order in writing require the owner, agent or manager of any group of specified mines or of all mines in a specified area to constitute a group Safety Committee in such manner and subject to such conditions as he may specify in the order.

Hence, the correct option is (C).

50. A universal milling machine have a table fitted with all motions and a dividing head with change gears so that it can perform any type of milling operation.

The worktable can move rapidly in three directions (vertical, horizontal and vertical), reduce the auxiliary time and increase productivity. The movement of the worktable in both horizontal and vertical directions is centrally controlled by a handle.

The operator can control the feeding motion of the two directions of the worktable with the handle.

A swivel joint for a pipe is often a threaded connection in between which at least one of the pipes is curved, often at an angle of 45 or 90 degrees.

Hence, the correct option is (C).

51. A 15 mm drilling machine means that it can drill a hole of a maximum diameter 15 mm.

A drilling machine comes in many shapes and sizes, from small hand-held power drills to bench mounted and finally floor-mounted models. They can perform operations other than drilling, such as countersinking, counterboring, reaming, and tapping large or small holes. Because the drilling machines can perform all of these operations, this chapter will also cover the types of drill bits, took, and shop formulas for setting up each operation.

Hence, the correct option is (A).

52. The cutting/machining time for which the tool has performed satisfactorily is termed as 'Tool Life'. The Tool is said to be not performing satisfactorily or tool life is said to be over if any one or more than one conditions are being observed while machining.

1) Poor surface finish is obtained.

2) Sudden increase in power and cutting force with chattering take place.

3) Overheating and funning due to friction starts.

Hence, the correct option is (D).

53. A fixture is a work-holding or support device used in the manufacturing industry. Fixtures are used to securely locate (position in a specific location or orientation) and support the work, ensuring that all parts produced using the fixture will maintain conformity and interchangeability.

Hence, the correct option is (B).

54. High-speed steel drills can be operated at about double the speed of high carbon steel drills. High-speed steel (HSS or HS) is a subset of tool steels, commonly used as cutting tool material.

It is often used in power-saw blades and drill bits. It is superior to the older high-carbon steel tools used extensively through the 1940s in that it can withstand higher temperatures without losing its temper (hardness). This property allows HSS to cut faster than high carbon steel, hence the name high-speed steel.

Hence, the correct option is (C).

55. At least 15% of the packed explosives are less effective than bulk explosives.

Bulk explosives; Explosives not individually packaged in a form usable in the field.

Includes ammonium nitrate-fuel oil, slurries, water gels, and other similar blasting agents, often loaded directly into blast holes from a bulk delivery truck.

Hence, the correct option is (B).

56. Deadtime of the instrument is the time required by an instrument for initial warming up.

It is defined as the time required by a measurement system to begin to respond to a change in the measurement. It is basically the time before the instrument begins to respond after the measurand has been changed.

Hence, the correct option is (B).

57. In electrical measuring instruments electrical energy is converted to mechanical energy.

Ammeter, Voltmeter, Ohmmeter, and Wattmeter are the example of the electrical measuring instrument. These instruments calculate or measure the value of electrical quantities, by converting them into mechanical quantities.

Hence, the correct option is (A).

58. The Torque weight ratio will be least in dynamometer instruments. The ratio of torque to the weight of the moving part of an instrument is known as a torque/weight ratio. It indexes the performance of the instrument. The higher value of the torque/weight ratio shows that the instrument has good performance. A dynamometer, or "dyno" for short, is a device for measuring force, a moment of force (torque), or power.

.Hence, the correct option is (A).

59. The vibrating-reed electrometer uses a capacitor that has a vibrating reed as one of its plates. The Movement of the reed changes the voltage across the capacitor.

A Frequency meter is an instrument that displays the frequency of a periodic electrical signal. Changes in the frequency to be measured cause a change in this balance that can be measured by the deflection of a pointer on a scale.

Hence, the correct option is (B).

60. The Scale of an instrument is the torque that deflects the pointer on a calibrated scale according to the electrical quantity passing through the instrument.

The deflecting torque causes the moving system and hence pointer attached to it moves from zero position to indicate electrical quantity being measured on a graduated scale.

Hence, the correct option is (C).

61. A good EIA report and review include assessment, mitigation measures terms of reference (TOR), prediction of the adverse effects of proposed actions and their mitigation using conventional and customized techniques, relevant and important information for decision making.

It does not tell about the project benefits.

A good EIA report and review include assessment, mitigation measures terms of reference (TOR), prediction of the adverse effects of proposed actions and their mitigation using conventional and customized techniques and relevant and important information for decision making.

Hence, the correct option is (B).

62. Depending on the EIA system, responsibility for producing an EIA will be assigned to one of two parties:

(1) The government agency or ministry.

(2) The project proponent.

If EIA laws permit, either party may opt to hire a consultant to prepare the EIA or handle specific portions of the EIA process, such as public participation or technical studies.

Hence, the correct option is (C).

63. Denitrification is the process that converts nitrate to nitrogen gas, thus removing bioavailable nitrogen and returning it to the atmosphere. Dinitrogen gas (N_2) is the ultimate end product of denitrification.

Hence, the correct option is (B).

64. In the process of rotating biological contractors, the large diameter corrugated plastic discs are mounted on a horizontal shaft and placed in a tank. The medium is slowly rotated with about 40 percent of the surface area always submerged in the flowing wastewater.

Hence, the correct option is (D).

65. India ranks 133rd in the world in terms of water availability per person per annum. It receives nearly 4 percent of the global precipitation. The per annum water availability in the country is reducing due to the increase in population.

Hence, the correct option is (D).

66. Groundwater is commonly accessed either through a bore or drilling well. A drilling well is a vertical shaft that is dug into the ground. In order to drill a well, we need to have permission from the government. The Government provides a 'take and use license' in most cases.

Hence, the correct option is (A).

67. The ovens used in gas chromatography must have maximum thermal gradients. The temperature must be uniform over the whole column. In gas chromatography, the mobile phase (or "moving phase") is a carrier gas, usually an inert gas such as helium or an unreactive gas such as nitrogen. Helium remains the most commonly used carrier gas in about 90% of instruments although hydrogen is preferred for improved separations.

Hence, the correct option is (C).

68. The unmarked component is a syringe. Hence, the unmarked component is a sample injection system. It is for the introduction of a sample into the flowing gas stream.

Hence, the correct option is (D).

69. The ratio between H.P of ventilation and H.P. of the fan shaft is the ratio of the mechanical output to the thermal input. Overall efficiency looks at entire systems from the initial input to the final output. Again it is the ratio of energy output to energy input.

Hence, the correct option is (D).

70. A mechanical efficiency is a dimensionless number that measures the effectiveness of a machine in transforming the power input to the device to power output. A machine is a mechanical linkage in which force is applied at one point, and the force does work moving a load at another point.

Hence, the correct option is (A).

71. The low-pressure system moves the ash mixed in water at a distance of 3 to 5 m/s in a sloped pump made of reinforced constituents and this movement is continuous. So, it has the ability to carry the ash for an approximate 500m distance. There is no requirement for any auxiliary source to move the ash mixed with water.

Hence, the correct option is (B).

72. The capacity of the low-pressure hydraulic ash handling system is 50 tonnes/hour at a speed of 3m/s. Since the ash produced is mixed in water and dumped, the water has the ability to dissolve and intake more amount of ash. And this mixture is spread throughout the sump.

Hence, the correct option is (C).

73. RDX stands for Royal Demolition eXplosive. It is also known as cyclonite or hexogen. The chemical name for RDX is 1,3,5-trinitro-1,3,5-triazine. It is a white powder and is very explosive. RDX is used as an explosive and is also used in combination with other ingredients in explosives.

Hence, the correct option is (D).

74. Xenon is also known as the stranger element. The element's name came from the Greek word Xenos, which means 'stranger'. Xenon belongs to the group of noble gases. Noble gases are very unreactive. However, in 1962, chemists have found that xenon can react with fluorine under special conditions, such as high pressure and high temperature.

Hence, the correct option is (C).

75. Steel is a non-combustible building material, but it is a good conductor of heat and hence, it is rapidly heated in case of a fire.

It is found that the Steel loses its tensile strength with the increase in the heat and yield stress of mild steel at 600°C is about one-third of its value at normal temperature. Hence, under intense fire, the unprotected steel beams sag unprotected Steel column buckle and the structure collapse.

Hence, the correct option is (D).

76. Aluminium is an excellent heat and electricity conductor. Aluminium also possesses poor fire-resisting properties. Hence, it's used is restricted to that structure that has very low fire risk.

Hence, the correct option is (B).

77. The land is said to be water-logged when the productivity of land gets affected and the crop root-zone gets deprived of proper aeration due to the flooding or high water table. It represents a saturated condition of the soil especially that of the crop root-zone with water. It also leads to the salinity of the soil.

Hence, the correct option is (A).

78. Very strongly alkaline soils (pH>9) and ultra-acidic soils (pH<3.5) are very rare. The USDA classifies soil pH for alkalinity as follows:

Denomination	pH range

Slightly alkaline	7.4 – 7.8
Moderately alkaline	7.9 – 8.4
Strongly alkaline	8.5 – 9.0
Very strongly alkaline	> 9.0

Hence, the correct option is (C).

79. Presence of excessive moisture lowers the temperature of the soil. In low temperatures the bacterial activities are retarded and their growth rates are also affected. It affects the soil-crop badly as soil microbial activity is disturbed.

Hence, the correct option is (A).

80. Water-logging occurs when there is too much water in a plant's root zone, which decreases the oxygen available to roots. Water-logging can be a major constraint to plant growth and production and, under certain conditions, will cause plant death.

By observing variations in the ground-water level is one of the ways of keeping a check on the problem. It can be done by measuring the depth of water levels at regular intervals in the wells dug in the area.

Hence, the correct option is (D).

81. The braided wire rope sling is comprised of several galvanised steel wire ropes, braided by hand. It offers a safety factor of 5. The braided sling is highly flexible, resistant and has a large grip width. It can be used for "basket handling". Braided wire slings are excellent for higher capacity lifts and can be either round or flat. One benefit of a braided sling is its ability to conform snugly to a load that's in a choker hitch. Because of the braided design, they also are better resistant to kinking.

Hence, the correct option is (A).

82. Alloy steel chains are often used because of their strength, durability, abrasion resistance and ability to conform to the shape of the loads on which they are used. These chains are manufactured and tested in accordance with ASTM (American Society for Testing and Maintenance) guidelines.

Hence, the correct option is (B).

83. Steel wire ropes are specified by nominal rope diameter in millimeters followed by the number of strands and the number of wires in a strand. A steel wire rope is made up of individual steel wires spun into a strand. A number of strands are closed over a central core thus producing a rope. The number and size of wires must offer the best compromise possible between large wires for maximum corrosion protection and resistance to abrasion, and smaller wires for the necessary flexibility and handling.

Hence, the correct option is (B).

84. An essential requirement of a good MH (Material Handling) system is storing materials utilizing minimum space.

Material Handling refers to activities, equipment, and procedures related to the moving, storing, protecting and controlling of materials in a system.

Hence, the correct option is (D).

85. The motor in close is used for collieries, the chemical plant is Flameproof type.

Flame-proof is the term used for motors that are certified for compliance with international standard International Electrotechnical Commission (IEC) 60079-1.

Hence, the correct option is (A).

86. A Totally Enclosed Fan-Cooled (TEFC) electric motor is a type of industrial electric motor with an enclosure that does not permit outside air to freely circulate through the interior of the motor. An external fan blows outside air over the frame of the motor to cool it.

Hence, the correct option is (B).

87. The motor enclosure used for industrial purposes is a Protected type.

An enclosure protects a motor from contaminants in the environment in which it is operating. In addition, the type of enclosure affects the cooling of the motor. Enclosures are categorized as either open or totally enclosed, and there are different types of enclosures within each category.

Hence, the correct option is (A).

88.

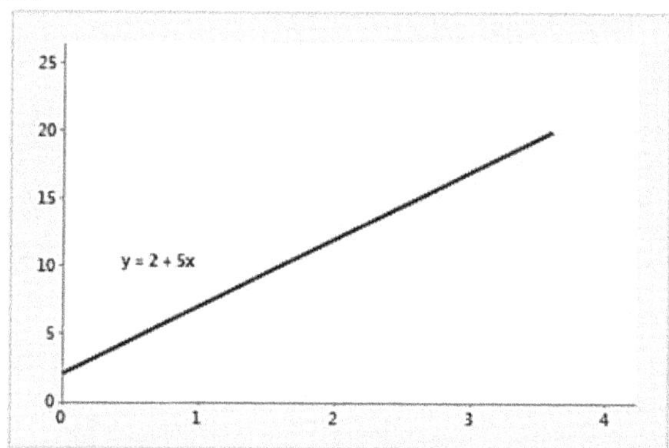

The coefficient (and slope) is positive 5.

The regression coefficients are a statically measure that is used to measure the average functional relationship between variables. In regression analysis, one variable is dependent and the other is independent. Also, it measures the degree of dependence of one variable on the other.

Hence, the correct option is (A).

89. Method of correlation involves determining the multiples or the individual constants, which can be further used for finding the probable values of unknowns. For finding these, a lot of conditions were established.

Hence, the correct option is (B).

90. The features in-laws of accidental errors include the tendency of small errors to be more frequent, positive and negative errors with equal frequency and making large errors occurrence impossible.

Hence, the correct option is (A).

91. Most probable value is equal to the arithmetic mean, in case all the taken weights are equal and in case of unequal weights, it is equal to the weighted arithmetic mean.

Hence, the correct option is (C).

92. SI unit of Luminous intensity is candela represented by cd. Luminous intensity is a Photometric quantity. The luminous intensity is a quantity for characterizing a light source. It is defined as the luminous flux per unit solid angle.

Hence, the correct option is (D).

93. The probability curve, which is established from the theory of probability, describes the features like relative frequency of the errors in the form of the curve. It is the basis for many mathematical derivations.

Hence, the correct option is (B).

94. MRP systems (I and II) help plan and optimize manufacturing production lines. The difference being, MRP II uses additional data from accounting records and sales for further analysis and forecasting of manufacturing requirements, are related to finance. MRP I stands for material requirements planning, while MRP II stands for manufacturing resource planning.

Hence, the correct option is (C).

95. The only lot size is considered in the inventory record file.

The Lot size refers to the quantity of an item ordered for delivery on a specific date or manufactured in a single production run. In other words, lot size basically refers to the total quantity of a product ordered for manufacturing.

Hence, the correct option is (A).

96. Water Safety Plans are an improved risk management tool designed to ensure the safety of drinking water through the use of a comprehensive risk assessment and risk management approach that encompasses all steps in water supply from catchment to consumer.

Hence, the correct option is (D).

97. Multiple frequencies are not used in the tracking system.

The sensitivity and reliability of position solutions using multiple frequencies are influenced by the individual signal performance in a challenging signal environment.

Hence, the correct option is (A).

98. In GPS relative positioning, the objective is to determine the coordinates of an unknown point with respect to another known point. Viscosity is the tendency of fluid friction. So, the viscous GPS technique is not a relative positioning technique.

Hence, the correct option is (B).

99. The real-time kinematic technique is having a high precision, which uses carrier phase measurements in the instantaneous positioning mode. It is considered as the most powerful GPS positioning technology.

Hence, the correct option is (D).

100. Kinematic positioning technique is considered as modern GPS technology. Real-time kinematic (RTK) positioning is a satellite navigation technique used to enhance the precision of position data derived from satellite-based positioning systems.

Hence, the correct option is (D).

Mock Test 04

General knowledge And Current Affairs

Q.1 The Mahanadi Coalfields Limited (MCL) has crossed how many million tonnes (MT) in coal production in the financial year of 2021-22?

A. 142 **B.** 157 **C.** 169 **D.** 175

Q.2 The territory of Porus who offered strong resistance to Alexander was situated between the rivers of:

A. Sutlej and Beas **B.** Jhelum and Chenab
C. Ravi and Chenab **D.** Ganga and Yamuna

Q.3 The Radcliffe line is a boundary between:

A. India and Pakistan
B. India and China
C. India and Myanmar
D. India and Afghanistan

Q.4 Who won the F1 Tuscan Grand Prix 2020?

A. Alexander Albon **B.** Valtteri Bottas
C. Lewis Hamilton **D.** None of these

Q.5 Name a clinical trial in which blood is transfused from recovered COVID-19 patients to a coronavirus patient who is in critical condition?

A. Plasma Therapy
B. Solidarity
C. Remdesivir
D. Hydroxychloroquine

Q.6 Which among the following department launched pan India 1000 SARS-CoV-2 RNA genome sequencing programme in collaboration with the national laboratories and clinical organization?

A. Department of Chemicals and Petrochemicals
B. Department for Science and Technology
C. Department of Health and Family Welfare
D. Department of Biotechnology

Q.7 The reservation for SC/STs in Lok Sabha, state assemblies have been extended by how much period?

A. 15 years **B.** 12 years **C.** 10 years **D.** 5 years

Q.8 The new committee system constitutes an improvement over the earlier committee system in so far as:

A. It assures representation to all the political parties in proportion to their strength in the Parliament
B. It enables the Parliament to examine the grants of all the ministries and departments in detail
C. It enables the Parliament to accept the demands of various ministries without scrutiny
D. None of the above

Q.9 Who invented the Hovercraft?

A. S. Sparrow **B.** O. Stricheg
C. T. Henman **D.** C. Cockerell

Q.10 National expenditure includes:

A. Consumption expenditure
B. Investment expenditure
C. Government expenditure
D. All of the above

Mine management, Legislation and General Safety

Q.11 Joint Management Councils are established in an organization that employs:

A. 100 employees
B. 300 employees
C. 400 employees
D. 500 employees or more

Q.12 ROI stands for:

A. Return on Insurance
B. Return on Investment
C. Rate on Insurance
D. Risk on Insurance

Q.13 Talent Management consists of:

(i) Performance Evaluations to identify potentials.

(ii) Psychological testing and assessment to determine capability gaps.

(iii) Training & development programs.

(iv) Project work & job experience to accelerate development.

A. i, ii, iii **B.** ii, iii, iv
C. i, ii, iii, iv **D.** Only i

Q.14 The break-even point represents:

A. The most economical level of operation of any industry
B. The time when the unit can run without loss and profit
C. The time when the industry will undergo loss
D. The time when the industry will undergo profit

Q.15 In the cost structure of a product, the selling price is determined by factors such as:

A. Sales turn over
B. Lowest competitive price
C. Various elements of the cost
D. All of the above

Q.16 Work-study is concerned with:

A. Improving the present method and finding the standard time
B. The motivation of workers
C. Improving production capability
D. Improving production planning and control

Q.17 The full form of CPM is _________

A. Critical Path Method
B. Control Path Method
C. Critical Plan Management
D. Control Path Management

Q.18 Accordingto the Mines Act 1952, the Calendar year means:

A. 1st Apr to 31st Mar
B. 1st Jan to 31st Dec
C. 1st Jan to 30th Sep
D. 1st Oct to 31st

Q.19 Register of annual return for the year is maintained in the form of

A. FORM Q **B.** FORM R
C. FORM S **D.** FORM T

Q.20 Register of the report of medical re-examination is maintained in the form of

A. FORM Q **B.** FORM R
C. FORM S **D.** FORM T

Q.21 Register of the second and final notice of medical by the medical board is maintained in the form of

A. FORM Q **B.** FORM R
C. FORM S **D.** FORM T

Q.22 Register of the notice of medical re-examination by the medical board is maintained in the form of

A. FORM Q **B.** FORM R
C. FORM S **D.** FORM T

Q.23 Record maintained by workmen's inspector is maintained in the form of

A. FORM G **B.** FORM R
C. FORM T **D.** FORM U

Q.24 Hazard communication in OSHA conducts ________.

A. Chemical analysis
B. Toxic exposure
C. Strength analysis
D. Hazard evaluations of the products

Q.25 The OSHA Form 300 is an_______log.

A. Injury **B.** Analysis
C. Finance **D.** Assistance

Q.26 Which ISO standard defines the effect of uncertainty on objectives for risk management?

A. 21000 **B.** 31000 **C.** 11000 **D.** 9000

Q.27 What is the main objective of risk assessment?

A. To evaluate hazard and minimize the risks
B. Remediation of contaminated sites
C. Hazard management
D. To know the source of pollutants

Q.28 The first aid room shall have a floor space of not less than___ .

A. 10 sq.m **B.** 14 sq.m **C.** 20 sq.m **D.** 18 sq.m

Q.29 The first aid room shall be in charge of a qualified medical practitioner where the number of persons ordinarily employed in a mine is more than:

A. 500 **B.** 1000 **C.** 250 **D.** 150

Q.30 Every person who suffers an injury during the course of work shall report for examination or treatment at the first aid room hospital or dispensary:

A. Before leaving the mine
B. Before entering the mine
C. After leaving the mine
D. None of these

Q.31 The first aid station shall be provided at the top of every shaft, in every workshop, at every other place, at every opencast working where more than persons___________are employed at any time.

A. 50 **B.** 25 **C.** 100 **D.** 150

Q.32 The first aid stations shall be constructed such that the provision of a first aid station within ....of another first aid station.

A. 100m **B.** 200m **C.** 300m **D.** 400m

Q.33 If the source of drinking water is not from a public water supply system. An inspector may by order in writing require the owner, agent, or manager of the mine to submit a certificate from a competent health authority or analysts to fitness of the water for human consumption within_________.

A. 7 days
B. 15 days
C. 3 days
D. At least possible delay

Q.34 Zero defects in manufacturing are:

A. A relevant goal only in electronic assembly
B. Readily achievable in all areas
C. The goal of TQM
D. An unobtainable and misleading idea

Q.35 The supply chain management philosophy emerged in which decade?

A. 1960s **B.** 1970s **C.** 1980s **D.** 1990s

Q.36 A __________ encompasses all activities associated with the flow and transformation of goods from the raw material stage, through to the end-user, as well as the associated information flows.

A. Production line **B.** Supply chain
C. Marketing channel **D.** Warehouse

Q.37 Which of the following is/are a typical question dealt with by an operation manager?

A. How much capacity will be needed in the months ahead?
B. What is a satisfactory location for a new facility?
C. How to motivate employees?
D. All of the above

Q.38 Contemporary supply chains should be fast and __________.

A. Lean　**B.** Agile
C. Interactive　**D.** Relevant

Q.39 The bullwhip effect:

A. Is an ineffective way to motivate warehouse employees
B. Applies to rodeos and has nothing to do with supply chain management
C. Refers to variability in demand orders among supply chain participants
D. None of the above

Q.40 The two key factors that have sparked much of the technological change affecting supply chains are __________ and __________.

A. EDI(Electronic Data interchange), ERP(Enterprise Resource Planning)
B. Computing power, ERP(Enterprise Resource Planning)
C. EDI(Electronic Data interchange), Internet
D. Computing power, Internet

Winning and Working

Q.41 Which of the following groups of states accounts for about 90% of the annual coal production in India?

A. Orissa, Madhya Pradesh, and Rajasthan
B. Jharkhand, Orissa and West Bengal
C. Madhya Pradesh, Tamil Nadu, and West Bengal
D. Jharkhand, Orissa and Madhya Pradesh

Q.42 Distinct texture shown by limestone is __________.

A. Sheeting　**B.** Lamination
C. Fossiliferous nature　**D.** Mud cracks

Q.43 Which type of limestone is non-marine in origin among the following?

A. Chalk
B. Kankar
C. Shelly-limestone
D. Argillaceous limestone

Q.44 The silicious sandstone which has been subjected to metamorphic action is called:

A. Moorum　**B.** Laterite
C. Quartzite　**D.** Dolomite

Q.45 For railway ballast, the stone should be:

A. Soft with a uniform texture
B. Hard, heavy, strong, and durable
C. Hard, tough, resistant to abrasion, and durable
D. Hard, dense, durable, tough, and easily workable

Q.46 When quarrying is to be done in hard stone and compact rocks, the usual method of quarrying is:

A. By wedging
B. By channeling machine
C. By blasting
D. All of these

Q.47 The dolomite bricks are:

A. Ordinary bricks
B. Acid refractory bricks
C. Basic refractory bricks
D. Neutral refractory bricks

Q.48 The most powerful explosive used in blasting is:

A. Blasting power　**B.** Dynamite
C. Guncotton　**D.** Cordite

Q.49 The Triaxial compression test was introduced by __________.

A. A. Casagrande and Karl Terzaghi
B. Mohr
C. Taylor
D. All of the above

Q.50 Which of the following strength test is commonly used in the laboratory?

A. Direct shear test
B. Confined compression test
C. Triaxial shear test
D. Unconfined shear test

Q.51 Which of the following outlet is provided at the base of the triaxial test apparatus?

A. Cell fluid inlet　**B.** Pore water outlet
C. Drainage outlet　**D.** All of the above

Q.52 How many elastic constants of a linear, elastic, isotropic material will be?

A. 2　**B.** 3　**C.** 1　**D.** 4

Q.53 How many elastic constants of a non-homogeneous, non-isotropic material will be?

A. 9　**B.** 15　**C.** 20　**D.** 21

Q.54 When too many people stand on a bridge it collapses, why?

A. Due to increase in stress
B. Due to overweight
C. Due to improper construction
D. Due to friction

Q.55 For a constant force, a rope breaks due to stress. Which of the following is useful to reduce stress?

A. Increase the length of the rope
B. Apply small force
C. Increase the cross-sectional area of the rope
D. Use a different material of rope

Q.56 Does total pressure take into the account force exerted by the fluid when it is in the dynamic motion?

A. Yes
B. No
C. Depends on the conditions
D. Depends on the type of Motion

Q.57 With rise in temperature, the Young's modulus of elasticity of a material

A. Increases
B. Decreases
C. Does not change
D. May increase or decrease

Q.58 A rolling contact bearing is specified as X307. Determine the series.
A. Extra light series **B.** Light series
C. Medium series **D.** Heavy series

Q.59 Extreme pressure causes _____ wear in the bearing parts.
A. Abrasive **B.** Corrosive
C. Pitting **D.** All of the above

Q.60 Scoring is a _______ phenomenon.
A. Stick-slip **B.** Fracture
C. Fatigue **D.** In-out

Surface environment, Mine Ventilation and Hazards

Q.61 The project proponents carry out the ______ process by assessing their project based upon a set of criteria determined by a designated agency.
A. Screening **B.** Elimination
C. Discussion **D.** None of the above

Q.62 Which of the following appears to contribute to global cooling rather than global warming?
A. Nitrous oxide
B. Aerosols
C. Methane
D. Chlorofluorocarbons

Q.63 What is true for the Scoping step?
1. It is a systematic exercise that establishes the boundaries of an EIA.
2. It clearly indicates what is relevant and what is not relevant within an EIA.
3. It serves as a work plan for the entire EIA process.

A. 1 and 2 **B.** 2 and 3
C. 1 and 3 **D.** All of the above

Q.64 What is Eutrophication?
A. Thermal change in water
B. Filling up of water body with aquatic plants due to excessive nutrients
C. Pollution of water due to solid waste
D. None of the above

Q.65 _______is a critical part of the EIA. It is mandated by legislation.
A. Public consultation
B. Media consultation
C. Communities consultation
D. None of the above

Q.66 TOR in EIA stands for;
A. Terms of reference **B.** Time of reaction
C. Team for reappeal **D.** None of the above

Q.67 What is meant by the development project's Areas of Influence?
1. The project environment is located outside the area of the overall project and extends from its boundaries to a distance of 500 meters.
2. The sector within which the EIA will be developed (Mining, Tourism, etc.).
3. The environmental impacts that will occur outside of the project due to water flow, migratory species, etc. Impact Assessment and Mitigation questions.

A. 1 and 2 **B.** Only 2 **C.** Only 3 **D.** Only 1

Q.68 Which process is employed to gain sufficient head for the wastewater?
A. Screening **B.** Pumping
C. Oxidation **D.** Fermentation

Q.69 What is the most commonly used coagulant?
A. Alum **B.** Ferric sulphate
C. Limestone **D.** Coal

Q.70 What is the intermediate zone composed of in aerobic-anaerobic ponds?
A. Algae **B.** Aerobic bacteria
C. Facultative bacteria **D.** Organic solids

Q.71 Nitrification efficiency is significantly suppressed as the temperature is ________.
A. Increased **B.** Decreased
C. Neutral **D.** Maintained

Q.72 Ventilation arising from the temperature difference between outside and inside takes place due to __________ effect.
A. Stack **B.** Stark **C.** Zeeman **D.** Spark

Q.73 The ventilation system which takes intake ventilating air to the lowest point of the district or face and allow it to travel to higher levels to ventilate the district before it goes to the return:
A. Ascential ventilation
B. Descential ventilation
C. Homotropal
D. Antitropal

Q.74 Natural ventilation pressure assists the fan ventilation pressure in case of:
A. Ascential ventilation
B. Descential ventilation
C. Homotropal
D. Antitropal

Q.75 When the air and mineral flow in the same direction the ventilation is called?
A. Ascential ventilation
B. Descential ventilation
C. Homotropal ventilation

D. Antitropal ventilation

Q.76 The effect of splitting the air in parallel is:

A. The overall resistance of mine increases
B. The overall resistance of mine decreases
C. The pressure produced by fan increases
D. The pressure produced by fan decreases

Q.77 Which medium is used to carry ash in the pneumatic ash handling system?

A. Conveyor belt **B.** Water trough
C. Air medium **D.** Chain belt

Q.78 Which system is noisy out of all the following ash handling systems?

A. Steam jet ash handling system
B. Mechanical ash handling system
C. Pneumatic ash handling system
D. Hydraulic ash handling system

Q.79 Which medium is used to carry ash in the hydraulic system?

A. Air **B.** Water
C. Steam **D.** Conveyor

Q.80 The apparatus used to administer pure oxygen to an unconscious person or affected by noxious gasses is_____.

A. Smoke helmet
B. Self-rescuer Reviving apparatus
C. SCBA
D. None of these

Mine Machineries, surveying and electricity

Q.81 Loads are usually classified into:

A. Payload and dead load
B. Unit load and bulk load
C. Pallet load and hoisting load
D. None of these

Q.82 Hoisting drum of a crane shall be made of:

A. Grey cast iron: grade 25 of IS: 210-1962
B. Cast steel: grade 2 of IS: 1030-1963
C. Mild steel IS: 226-1962
D. All of the above

Q.83 What are bulk loads?

A. Lump of material
B. Single rigid mass
C. Homogeneous particles
D. Heterogeneous particles

Q.84 Rope reeving is used to indicate:

A. The relative direction of twist in the steel wire
B. The minimum breaking load of a rope
C. The payload is lifted on two, four or six or eight parts of the rope
D. None of these

Q.85 Impact idlers are used in a belt conveyor:

A. At the loading points
B. At the return point
C. At an interval of 15 m on a conveyor run
D. None of the above

Q.86 Ash is abrasive as well as dusty. Which conveyor will be preferred for its handling?

A. Belt conveyor
B. Flight conveyor
C. Drag chain conveyor
D. Screw conveyor

Q.87 Based on air pressures, pneumatic conveying systems may be classified as:

A. Dilute phase and dense phase
B. Blow vessels and air slides
C. Positive pressure, negative pressure, combined positive-negative system
D. None of the above

Q.88 The choice of appropriate type of pneumatic conveying system depends upon:

A. Bulk density and particle size
B. Flowability
C. Abrasiveness
D. All of the above

Q.89 Lay of steel wire ropes classifies them into:

A. Regular Lay, Lang's Lay, Reverse Lay
B. Warrington compound and non-spinning
C. Locked coil and flattened
D. None of these

Q.90 Consider the following statements.

i. Capacity of the pump
ii. Number of pump units
iii. Discharge condition

The selection of a particular type of pump depends on which of the following:

A. i, ii, iii **B.** i only **C.** ii, iii **D.** i, iii

Q.91 The speed at which the centrifugal pump runs (in r.p.m) is ___________.

A. 200 **B.** 300 **C.** 500 **D.** 1200

Q.92 The maximum efficiency of a centrifugal pump is ___________.

A. 40% to 50% **B.** 55% to 60%
C. 75% to 93% **D.** 100%

Q.93 Which of the following describes the work done by the method of correlates?

A. Reducing the mean work
B. Neglecting the arithmetic work
C. Increasing the arithmetic work
D. Reducing the arithmetic work

Q.94 Clients use which protocol to discover SMI Agents on Storage Area Network?

A. SLP (Service Location Protocol)
B. AGP(Agent Discovery Protocol)
C. SMIP (SMI Protocol)
D. None of the mentioned

Q.95 The centrifugal pump has a _____ flow.
A. Variable
B. Uniform
C. Continuous
D. Constant

Q.96 Bill of material structure is used to:
A. Set requirements
B. Calculate due dates
C. Calculate manpower requirements
D. All of the above

Q.97 Just in time manufacturing philosophy emphasizes on:
A. Man power
B. Manufacturing
C. Profit
D. Inventory

Q.98 Forecasting is used for:
A. Dependent demand items
B. Independent demand items
C. Only items
D. None of the above

Q.99 CRP takes material requirements from MRP and converts to:
A. Standard hours of manpower
B. Standard hours of machine
C. Standard hours of load
D. All of the above

Q.100 Capacity planning is concerned with:
A. How many machines required
B. How much labour required
C. How many products produced
D. All of the above

// Smart Answer Sheet //

Correct Percentage of students who answered correctly. **Skipped** Percentage of students who skipped.

Q.	Ans.	Correct	Skipped	Q.	Ans.	Correct	Skipped	Q.	Ans.	Correct	Skipped	Q.	Ans.	Correct	Skipped	Q.	Ans.	Correct	Skipped	Q.	Ans.	Correct	Skipped
1	B	19.88 %	4.76 %	18	B	69.31 %	1.13 %	35	C	79.61 %	0.0 %	52	A	62.56 %	1.27 %	69	A	64.21 %	1.3 %	86	C	64.75 %	1.6 %
2	B	52.84 %	1.23 %	19	D	56.68 %	1.16 %	36	B	79.52 %	0.0 %	53	D	47.19 %	1.92 %	70	C	49.66 %	1.32 %	87	C	82.72 %	0.0 %
3	A	82.28 %	0.0 %	20	C	29.32 %	3.56 %	37	D	79.48 %	0.0 %	54	A	76.71 %	0.0 %	71	B	45.73 %	1.37 %	88	D	65.58 %	1.29 %
4	C	52.55 %	1.04 %	21	B	23.77 %	4.68 %	38	B	47.07 %	1.16 %	55	C	86.8 %	0.0 %	72	A	60.34 %	1.2 %	89	A	45.34 %	1.19 %
5	A	55.6 %	1.5 %	22	A	16.16 %	3.66 %	39	C	43.77 %	1.09 %	56	B	82.1 %	0.0 %	73	A	13.69 %	4.7 %	90	A	65.85 %	1.06 %
6	D	53.82 %	1.29 %	23	D	18.28 %	4.21 %	40	D	88.01 %	0.0 %	57	B	55.52 %	1.07 %	74	A	53.14 %	1.14 %	91	C	87.43 %	0.0 %
7	C	45.45 %	1.99 %	24	D	59.74 %	1.5 %	41	B	83.04 %	0.0 %	58	C	42.17 %	1.02 %	75	C	79.82 %	0.0 %	92	C	53.48 %	1.59 %
8	B	63.34 %	1.36 %	25	A	54.49 %	1.37 %	42	C	24.26 %	4.63 %	59	B	51.29 %	1.11 %	76	B	62.86 %	1.82 %	93	D	87.71 %	0.0 %
9	D	62.28 %	1.99 %	26	B	54.51 %	1.72 %	43	B	44.59 %	1.53 %	60	A	88.14 %	0.0 %	77	C	59.24 %	1.75 %	94	A	27.97 %	3.48 %
10	D	77.36 %	0.0 %	27	A	68.19 %	1.03 %	44	C	54.11 %	1.73 %	61	A	60.62 %	1.17 %	78	C	85.72 %	0.0 %	95	C	62.29 %	1.73 %
11	D	53.44 %	1.2 %	28	A	20.72 %	3.27 %	45	D	76.06 %	0.0 %	62	B	28.17 %	5.0 %	79	B	82.94 %	0.0 %	96	A	65.38 %	1.86 %
12	B	67.6 %	1.96 %	29	B	25.36 %	4.02 %	46	C	40.06 %	1.34 %	63	D	59.73 %	1.13 %	80	B	86.49 %	0.0 %	97	D	61.22 %	1.41 %
13	C	49.14 %	1.06 %	30	A	48.21 %	1.75 %	47	C	68.89 %	1.99 %	64	B	57.09 %	1.65 %	81	B	62.51 %	1.24 %	98	B	76.29 %	0.0 %
14	B	66.42 %	1.05 %	31	A	14.58 %	3.82 %	48	C	85.68 %	0.0 %	65	A	41.55 %	1.29 %	82	D	28.27 %	4.03 %	99	D	42.91 %	1.76 %
15	D	40.87 %	1.43 %	32	C	58.85 %	1.83 %	49	A	49.3 %	1.24 %	66	A	80.16 %	0.0 %	83	B	89.37 %	0.0 %	100	D	61.59 %	1.25 %
16	A	86.32 %	0.0 %	33	D	69.91 %	1.36 %	50	C	85.75 %	0.0 %	67	D	13.2 %	3.45 %	84	C	85.97 %	0.0 %				
17	A	77.94 %	0.0 %	34	C	87.08 %	0.0 %	51	D	63.25 %	1.41 %	68	B	48.77 %	1.72 %	85	D	49.76 %	1.68 %				

//Hints and Solutions//

1. The Mahanadi Coalfields Limited (MCL) has crossed 157 million tonnes (MT) in coal production in the financial year of 2021-22. It has become the leading coal-producing company in the country.

Mahanadi Coalfields Limited is one of the major coal-producing companies in India. It is one of the eight subsidiaries of Coal India Limited. Mahanadi Coalfields Limited was carved out of South Eastern Coalfields Limited. It was headquartered in Sambalpur. It was founded in 1992.

Hence, the correct option is (B).

2. The territory of Porus who offered strong resistance to Alexander was situated between the rivers of Jhelum and Chenab.

Porus was an ancient Indian king, whose territory spanned the region between the Hydaspes (Jhelum River) and Acesines (Chenab River), in the Punjab region of the Indian subcontinent. He is credited to have been a legendary warrior with exceptional skills. Porus fought against Alexander the Great in the Battle of the Hydaspes (326 BC), thought to be fought at the site of modern-day Mong, Punjab, which is now part of Pakistan.

Hence, the correct option is (B).

3. The Radcliffe Line became the international border between India and Pakistan (which also included what is now Bangladesh) during the partition of India. The line divided Bengal into Indian held West Bengal and East Bengal which became East Pakistan in 1956.

Hence, the correct option is (A).

4. Lewis Hamilton (Mercedes-Great Britain) has won the Formula One Tuscan Grand Prix 2020 held at Mugello Circuit, Italy. This was his 6th win of the season and the 90th F1 win of his career.

Hence, the correct option is (C).

5. Plasma Therapy or Convalescent Plasma Therapy is a clinical trial in which blood is transfused from recovered COVID-19 patients to a coronavirus patient who is in critical condition. Plasma is the liquid portion of blood that remains when all red and white blood cells and platelets have been removed. It was over a hundred years ago that Emil Behring was awarded the first Nobel prize for physiology and medicine for his work demonstrating that plasma could be used to treat diphtheria.

Hence, the correct option is (A).

6. Harsh Vardhan, Union Minister of Health and Family Welfare announced the completion of Pan-India Genome Sequencing of SARS-CoV-2 RNA Genome Sequencing programme. He reviewed the COVID-19 activities of the Department of Biotechnology(DBT), Biotechnology Industry Research Assistance Council (BIRAC) and DBT-Autonomous Institutions (AIs) in the meeting with DBT. He also launched the establishment of Five COVID-19 Bio Repositories by the DBT at Faridabad, Bhubaneshwar, New Delhi, Pune and Bangalore.

Hence, the correct option is (D).

7. The Union Cabinet on December 4, 2019, approved a proposal to extend the reservation for SCs and STs in the Lok Sabha and the state assemblies for another 10 years. The reservation for these categories in the Lok Sabha and the assemblies was to expire on January 25, 2020. The government will bring a bill to extend the reservation in this session. While reservation for Scheduled Castes and Scheduled Tribes in the legislature is carried out through constitutional amendments, similar reservation in jobs for these categories is decided by respective state governments.

Hence, the correct option is (C).

8. The new committee system constitutes an improvement over the earlier committee system in so far as it enables the Parliament to examine the grants of all the ministries and departments in detail.

The origin of the Committee system in India can be traced back to the Constitutional Reforms of 1919. Standing Committees are permanent and regular committees which are constituted from time to time in pursuance of the provisions of an Act of Parliament or Rules of Procedure and Conduct of Business In Lok Sabha.

Hence, the correct option is (B).

9. Christopher Cockerell invented the Hovercraft in 1955.

In 1955, British inventor and engineer Christopher Sydney Cockerell invented a swift water-transport vehicle that was not quite a boat, not quite a plane, but a hybrid of sorts called the hovercraft.

Hence, the correct option is (D).

10. The total level of expenditure in a national economy is equivalent to its total level of output and the total level of income is known as 'National expenditure'. It includes all types of expenditures from consumption to investment including the ones done by the government.

Hence, the correct option is (D).

11. Joint Management Councils are established in an organization that employs 500 employees or more. The Second Five Year Plan recommended the setting up of joint councils of management consisting of representatives of workers and management.

A joint council or committee representing employer and employees that discuss working conditions, wages, etc., within a plant or business.

Hence, the correct option is (D).

12. ROI stands for "Return on Investment".

Return on Investment (ROI) is a performance measure used to evaluate the efficiency of an investment or compare the efficiency of a number of different investments. ROI tries to directly measure the amount of return on a particular investment, relative to the investment's cost.

Hence, the correct option is (B).

13. Talent management is an organization's commitment to recruit, hire, retain, and develop the most talented and superior employees available in the job market. So, talent management is a useful term when it describes an organization's commitment to hire, manage, develop, and retain talented employees.

Hence, the correct option is (C).

14. The break-even point represents the time when the unit can run without loss and profit.

The breakeven point is the level of production at which the costs of production equal the revenues for a product. In investing, the breakeven point is said to be achieved when the market price of an asset is the same as its original cost.

Hence, the correct option is (B).

15. In the cost structure of a product, the selling price is determined by factors such as

- Sales turn over
- Lowest competitive price
- Other elements of the cost

The cost structure is the proportion of a company's fixed and variable costs in relation to its overall operation cost. A product cost structure has variable costs, such as materials, supplies, and commissions. A product cost structure's fixed costs usually include manufacturing overhead, such as rent and equipment.

Hence, the correct option is (D).

16. Work-study is concerned with Improving the present method and finding the standard time. The aim of the work-study is to determine the best method of performing each operation and to eliminate wastage so that production increases with less fatigue. The work-study is also used in determining the standard time that a qualified worker should take to perform the operation when working at a normal place.

Hence, the correct option is (A).

17. The full form of CPM is the Critical Path Method. CPM networks are mainly used for those projects for which a fairly accurate estimate of time of completion can be made for each activity. The critical path method (CPM) is a project modeling technique that's used by project managers to find important deadlines and deliver a project on time. In a project, the critical path is the longest distance between the start and the finish, including all the tasks and their duration. Once a critical path is determined, we can have a clear picture of the project's actual schedule.

Hence, the correct option is (A).

18. "Calendar year" means a year from the first day of January to the thirty-first day of December.

The calendar year, as the name implies, follows the structure of a standard calendar and begins on January 1. A fiscal year lasts for the same duration of 365 days but can begin any time as long as it ends a year later. Some companies opt to structure their fiscal years around financial reporting deadlines, begin the fiscal year at the end of tax season or devise another scheme that makes tracking money more convenient.

Hence, the correct option is (B).

19. Register of annual return for the year is maintained in the FORM T.

The registration of annual return is carried out on or before the 20th day of February every year, the manager of every mine shall submit to the Chief Inspector annual returns in respect of the preceding calendar year in FORM T.

Hence, the correct option is (D).

20. The Appellate Medical Board shall medically examine the appellant in accordance with the standard laid down in FORM P for initial medical examination of workers already in employment as well as periodical medical examination and in accordance with the standard laid down FORM P-I for initial medical examination of the persons to employed and shall issue to the manager of the mine concerned and to the appellant a medical certificate in FORM S.

Hence, the correct option is (C).

21. Register of the second and final notice of medical by the medical board is maintained in the form of FORM R. A person, who for any reasonable cause, fails to submit himself for a medical re-examination shall be given another notice in FORM R in a similar manner.

Hence, the correct option is (B).

22. Register of the notice of medical re-examination by the medical board is maintained in the FORM Q.

The manager shall arrange to have the appellant medically re-examined by the Appellate Medical Board within thirty days of the receipt of the Appeal and shall give to the Appellant fifteen days prior notice of the medical re-examination by the Appellate Medical Board in FORM Q.

Hence, the correct option is (A).

23. The Workmen's Inspector shall record a full report of the matters ascertained as a result of his inspection in an interleaved paged and bound register kept for the purpose in the mine in FORM U. The Workmen's Inspector making the entry in the register aforesaid shall duly sign such entries with the date and take a copy of the entries for his record.

Hence, the correct option is (D).

24. Hazard communication in OSHA (Occupational Safety and Health Administration) conducts hazard evaluations of the products.

Hazard communication standard requires manufacturers and importers of hazardous materials to conduct hazard evaluations of the products they manufacture or import. If a product is found to be hazardous under the terms of the standard, the manufacturer or importer must so indicate on containers of the material, and the first shipment of the material to a new customer must include Material Safety Data Sheets (MSDS).

Hence, the correct option is (D).

25. The OSHA Form 300 is an injury/illness log, with a separate line entry for each recordable injury or illness. The events include work-related deaths, injuries, and illnesses other than minor injuries that require only first aid treatment and that do not involve medical treatment, loss of consciousness, restriction of work, or transfer to another job.

Hence, the correct option is (A).

26. (International Organization for Standardization) ISO 31000 defines the effect of uncertainty on objectives for risk management.

Risk management – guidelines, provides principles, a framework, and a process for managing risk. It can be used by any organization regardless of its size, activity or sector.

Using ISO 31000 can help organizations increase the likelihood of achieving objectives, improve the identification of opportunities and threats, and effectively allocate and use resources for risk treatment.

Hence, the correct option is (B).

27. The main objective of risk assessment is to evaluate hazards and minimize the risks.

The aim of the risk assessment process is to evaluate hazards, then remove that hazard or minimize the level of its risk by adding control measures, as necessary. By doing so, we can create a safer and healthier workplace.

Hence, the correct option is (A).

28. The first-aid room shall have a floor space of not less than 10 sq.m and shall contain at least the equipment specified in the second schedule.

At every mine employing more than 150 persons on any one day of the preceding calendar year, there shall be provided and maintained in good order a suitable first-aid room. The first-aid room shall be situated at a convenient place on the surface of the mine and shall be used only for first-aid work.

Hence, the correct option is (A).

29. The first-aid room shall be in charge of a qualified medical practitioner, where the number of persons ordinarily employed in a mine is more than 1000, such medical practitioner shall be a whole-time employee at the mine.

Hence, the correct option is (B).

30. Every person who suffers an injury during the course of work shall report for examination or treatment at the first aid room, hospital or dispensary, as the case may be, before leaving the mine, irrespective of first-aid having been rendered at or near the place of work.

Hence, the correct option is (A).

31. At every mine, there shall be provided and maintained first-aid equipment, at conveniently accessible stations where injured persons may receive first-aid treatment as follows:

(i) at the top of every shaft or incline where men or material are normally wound or hauled.

(ii) in every workshop.

(iii) at every screening plant and loading place.

(iv) at every other place where more than 50 persons are employed at any one time.

Hence, the correct option is (A).

32. In every opencast working, one first-aid station for every 50 persons or part thereof, employed at any one time.

Below ground, one first-aid station must be:

(i) at the bottom of every shaft where men or material are normally wound, and at or near every plant.

(ii) in or at the entrance to every district or section of the mine.

Provided that nothing in this sub-rule shall be construed to require the provision of a first aid station within 300 meters of another first-aid station.

Hence the correct option is (C).

33. As in Health and Sanitation Provisions,

If the source of drinking water is not from a public water supply system, an Inspector may by ordering in writing require the owner, agent, or manager of the mine to submit with the least possible delay a certificate from a competent health authority or analyst as to the fitness of the water for human consumption.

Hence, the correct option is (D).

34. Zero defects in manufacturing are the goal of total quality management (TQM).

Total quality management (TQM) is the continual process of detecting and reducing or eliminating errors in manufacturing, streamlining supply chain management, improving the customer experience and ensuring that employees are up to speed with training.

Hence, the correct option is (C).

35. The term "supply chain management" was first coined by Keith Oliver in 1980s. However, the concept of a supply chain in management was of great importance long before, in the early 20th century, especially with the creation of the assembly line.

Hence, the correct option is (C).

36. Supply chain management includes all methods to change raw materials to final products. It is the management of the flow of services and goods. Encompasses the planning and management of all activities involved in sourcing and procurement, conversion, and all logistics management activities. importantly, it also includes coordination and collaboration with channel partners, which can be suppliers, intermediaries, third-party service providers, and customers. In essence, SCM integrates supply and demand management within and across companies.

Hence, the correct option is (B).

37. The Operations Manager's role is mainly to implement the right processes and practices across the organization. The specific duties of an Operations Manager include formulating strategy, improving performance, procuring material and resources, and securing compliance.

Hence, the correct option is (D).

38. Contemporary supply chains should be fast and agile. The concept of agility was given by (Goldman et al.1995). It means "readiness to change", from a business perspective, agility is defined as a strategy that is more responsive in a volatile market place, where this strategy is totally demand-driven. As consumers buying patterns are changing at a very rapid pace, so do the whole supply chain management changes. The fundamental drivers of the agile supply chain are Speed, Cost, and Efficiency. Agile supply chains are based on sensitivity to consumer demand. Here, sensitivity refers to the ultimate consumer demand, in terms of volatility of demand.

Hence, the correct option is (B).

39. The bullwhip effect refers to variability in demand orders among supply chain participants.

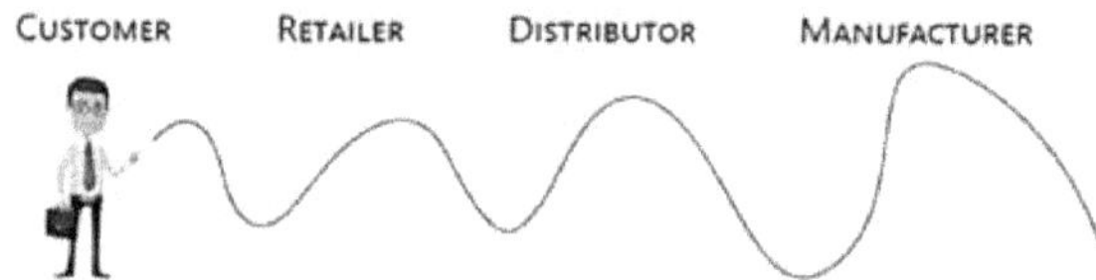

Imagine a person having a long whip in his hand, and if he gives a little nudge to the whip at the handle, it creates little movements in the parts closest to the handle, but parts further away would move more in an increasing fashion.

Similarly, in the supply chain world, the end customers have the whip handle and they create a little movement in the demand which travels up the supply chain in an increasing fashion. As we move away from the customer, we can see bigger movements. On average, there are six to seven inventory points between the end customer and raw material supplier.

Hence, the correct option is (C).

40. The two key factors that have sparked much of the technological change affecting supply chains are Computing power and the Internet. Information technologies (IT) have the greatest impact on supply chain coordination by eliminating information delays and distortions, reducing transaction costs, and, ultimately, enabling e- collaboration, which is defined as business-to-business interaction facilitated by the Internet.

Hence, the correct option is (D).

41. Jharkhand, Orissa, and West Bengal account for about 90% of the annual coal production in India.

Jharkhand has 83.15 billion tonnes of coal reserves. It is located in north-east India, the state of Jharkhand top the list of India's coal reserves. The state's main coal-mining centers are Jharia, Bokaro, Aurangabad, Giridh, Dhanbad, Ramgarh, Karanpu, and Hutar.

Nine coal mines of Orissa are among the 41 coal blocks in the country to be auctioned for commercial mining. The mines are Chendipada I, Chendipada II, Machhakata, Mahanadi, Radhikapur (East), Radhikapur (West), Brahmanbil & Kardabahal, Kuraloi (A) North, and Phuljhari (East & West).

West Bengal carries about 11 percent of the total coal reserves of India. The deposits are found in Bardhman, Darjeeling, Bankura, Jalpaiguri, and Puruliya districts of the state. Raniganj coalfield is the most important coal reserve and mining coalfield of West Bengal.

- Jharkhand – 83.15 billion tonnes.
- Orissa – 79.30 billion tonnes.
- West Bengal – 31.67 billion tonnes.

Hence, the correct option is (B).

42. The Distinct texture is shown by limestone is fossiliferous nature.

In view of the diverse ways in which the limestones are formed, these rocks show a variety of textures. The most important texture feature of limestone is its fossiliferous nature.

Fossiliferous Limestone is formed by various shells and skeletal fossils. Fossiliferous limestone is any type of limestone, made mostly of calcium carbonate ($CaCO_3$) in the form of the minerals calcite or aragonite, which contains an abundance of fossils or fossil traces.

Hence, the correct option is (C).

43. Kankar is a common nodular or concretionary form of carbonate material formed by the evaporation of subsoil water rich in calcium carbonate just near the soil surface. It is a non-marine in origin. Travertine, tufa, caliche, chalk, and micrite are all varieties of limestone. Limestone has rich fossil content.

Hence, the correct option is (B).

44. The silicious sandstone which has been subjected to metamorphic action is called quartzite.

Siliceous rock is defined as any group of sedimentary rocks that consist largely or almost entirely of silicon dioxide (SiO_2), either as quartz or as amorphous silica and cristobalite.

Metamorphism occurs when solid rock changes in composition and/or texture without the mineral crystals melting, which is how igneous rock is generated. Rock texture is changed by heat, confining pressure, and a type of pressure called directed stress.

Hence, the correct option is (C).

45. For railway ballast, the stones beneath the track must be hard, dense, durable, tough, and easily workable to bear huge stresses.

Ballast is the name for the 'stones' beneath the track. This aggregate forms the trackbed and supports the track. It also helps with drainage, so rainwater can drain away rather than pooling, and preventing vegetation growth, which could destabilize the track and be a hazard for anyone working on the railway.

Hence, the correct option is (D).

46. Removing rock, sand, gravel, or other minerals from the ground is done by blasting.

Quarrying is the process of removing rock, sand, gravel, or other minerals from the ground in order to use them to produce materials for construction or other uses. By far the bulk of rock excavated in mining globally is broken by drilling and blasting. Mining is the largest consumer of civil explosives.

Hence, the correct option is (C).

47. The dolomite bricks are basic refractory bricks.

Dolomite brick is made as refractory products from calcined dolomite sand. A refractory brick is built primarily to withstand high temperature, but will also usually have a low thermal conductivity for greater energy efficiency.

Hence, the correct option is (C).

48. The most powerful explosive used in blasting is guncotton.

Guncotton or nitrocellulose (also known as trinitrocellulose and cellulose nitrate) is a mild explosive, used in rockets, propellants, printing ink bases, leather finishing, and celluloid (a mixture of nitrocellulose and camphor; first used to manufacture billiard balls).

Hence, the correct option is (C).

49. The triaxial compression test was first introduced in the U.S.A by A. Casagrande and Karl Terzaghi in 1936-37.

Triaxial tests are widely used in geotechnical engineering both in soil and rock mechanics. Specimens are axially loaded to failure while a confining pressure is constantly applied. As a result, the behavior of geomaterials is investigated in a three-dimensional stress state.

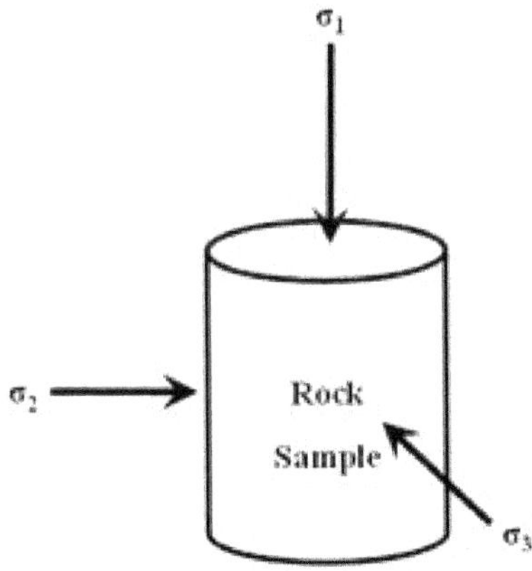

Hence, the correct option is (A).

50. The triaxial test is one of the most commonly used in the research laboratory. The triaxial test is one of the most versatile and widely performed geotechnical laboratory tests, allowing the shear strength and stiffness of soil and rock to be determined for use in geotechnical design.

Hence, the correct option is (C).

51. Three outlet connections are generally provided through the base of the test apparatus: cell fluid test, pore water outlet from the bottom of the specimen and the drainage outlet from the bottom of the specimen.

Hence, the correct option is (D).

52. There will be two elastic constants of a linear, elastic, isotropic material.

Isotropic materials have the same properties in all directions. The number of independent elastic constants for such materials is 2. out of E, G, K, and μ, if any two constants are known for any linear elastic and isotropic material then the rest two can be derived. Examples are steel, aluminium, copper, gold.

Hence, the correct option is (A).

53. Non-isotropic or anisotropic materials have different properties in different directions. They show non-homogeneous behaviour. The number of elastic constants is 21.

Hence, the correct option is (D).

54. When too many people stand on a bridge it collapses due to an increase in stress.

Stress is the force per unit area experienced by the body and strength is the ability to withstand the stress. When stress becomes greater than strength, accidents happen.

Hence, the correct option is (A).

55. Stress = Force/Area,

For a constant force, if the area is small, stress is large. If the area is large, stress is small. Therefore by increasing the cross-sectional area stress can be reduced considerably.

Hence, the correct option is (C).

56. Total pressure does not take into the account force exerted by the fluid when it is in dynamic motion.

The total pressure is defined only for the static fluid at rest. There is no dynamic component as no motion is involved.

Hence, the correct option is (B).

57. With rise in temperature, Young's modulus of elasticity of a material decreases.

Young's modulus shows rigidity of the material. when temperature increase then material starts to become soft. Therefore elasticity decreases with rise in temperature.

Hence, the correct option is (B).

58. A rolling contact bearing specified as X307 belongs to the medium series.

A rolling contact bearing is usually designated by three or four digits. The meaning of these digits is as follows:

(i) The last two digits indicate the bore diameter of the bearing in mm (bore diameter divided by 5). For example, XX07 indicates a bearing of 35 mm bore diameter.

(ii) The third digit from the right indicates the series of the bearing. The numbers used to indicate the series are as follows:

Extra light series –1, Light series – 2, Medium series – 3, Heavy series – 4

For example, X307 indicates a medium series bearing with a bore diameter of 35 mm.

(iii) The fourth digit and sometimes fifth digit from the right specifies the type of rolling-contact bearing. For example, the digit 6indicates deep groove ball bearings.

Hence, the correct option is (C).

59. Extreme pressure causes Corrosive wear in the bearing parts. Corrosive wear occurs when the contact surfaces chemically react with the environment and form reaction layers on their surfaces, layers that will be worn off by the mechanical action of the interacting contact surfaces.

Hence, the correct option is (B).

60. Scoring is a stick-slip phenomenon. Stick-slip can be described as surfaces alternating between sticking to each other and sliding over each other, with a corresponding change in the force of friction.

Hence, the correct option is (A).

61. The project proponents carry out the Screening process by assessing their project based upon a set of criteria determined by a designated agency.

Screening is the first stage of the EIA process which results in a key EIA decision, namely to either conduct the assessment (based on the likely significant impacts) or not conduct it (in the anticipated absence of such impacts).

Hence, the correct option is (A).

62. Aerosols contribute to global cooling rather than global warming.

Aerosols are minute particles that suspended in the atmosphere. Most aerosols are brighter in color and they reflect sunlight back to space. Thus they help in cooling the Earth.

Hence, the correct option is (B).

63. Scoping is the process of identifying the key environmental issues and is perhaps the most important step in an EIA.

The purpose of scoping is to focus the environmental impact issues to ensure that useful and relevant results will be obtained and to determine the parameters and boundaries of the assessment. The geographical area to be covered by the EIA may need to be much greater than just the local area in which the project is to be located. Ideally, a scoping exercise should involve public participation or consultation to make sure that those issues that are important to the public are addressed and considered at an early stage. This can allow for project design changes to accommodate them. It will be seen in the discussion of procedures that public consultation and participation frequently occur too late, if at all, with subsequent adverse effects for the environment, or for the project itself. Scoping can be considered as having three main components focusing on technical, political, and social aspects.

Hence, the correct option is (D).

64. Eutrophication is the process of excessive accumulation of nutrients in water bodies such as lakes and ponds and subsequent proliferation of algae and aquatic plants. This is a serious issue in many areas. Because the bloom of algae and plant life depletes oxygen in the water and threatens the existence of other aquatic life.

Hence, the correct option is (B).

65. Public consultation is a critical part of the EIA. It is mandated by legislation.

Public consultation is a process that involves the public in providing their views and feedback on a proposal to consider in the decision-making.

Hence, the correct option is (A).

66. TOR in EIA stands for Terms of reference.

TOR or Terms of Reference is a document produced by the authority conducting the EIA study. It is formed during Scoping, the second stage in the EIA process. TOR is an important document in the process of EIA because it sets the guidelines for the study.

Hence, the correct option is (A).

67. The term 'Area of influence' is understood as such area where significant environmental impacts caused by project performance are evident on physical, biotic, and socioeconomic components, in each component of such environment.

Hence, the correct option is (D).

68. Pumping facilities may be employed to gain sufficient head for the wastewater to flow through the treatment works to the point of final disposal. Pumping is also generally required for recirculation of all or part of the flow around certain units within the plant.

Hence, the correct option is (B).

69. The most commonly used coagulant is alum.

Sedimentation using chemical coagulation has been implied mainly to pre-treatment of industrial or process wastewaters and removal of phosphorus from domestic wastewaters. Alum is mostly used as it is cheap and easily available.

Hence, the correct option is (A).

70. Facultative bacteria is the intermediate zone composed of aerobic-anaerobic ponds. A facultative anaerobe is an organism that makes ATP by aerobic respiration if oxygen is present, but is capable of switching to fermentation if oxygen is absent.

Aerobic-anaerobic ponds consist of three zones:

1. A surface zone of algae and aerobic bacteria in a symbiotic association.
2. An intermediate zone populated with facultative bacteria (aerobic or anaerobic).
3. An anaerobic bottom zone where settled organic solids are decomposed by anaerobic bacteria.

Hence, the correct option is (C).

71. Nitrification efficiency is significantly suppressed as the temperature decreases.

Two important considerations in nitrification are the maintenance of a proper pH and temperature. Nitrification is a very temperature-sensitive system and the efficiency is significantly suppressed as the temperature decreases.

Nitrification is the process by which ammonia is converted to nitrites and then nitrates. This process naturally occurs in the environment, where it is carried out by specialized bacteria.

Hence, the correct option is (B).

72. Ventilation arising from the temperature difference between outside and inside takes place due to the stack effect. When the temperature of the inside air is higher than the outside air, warmer air passes through the opening situated in the upper part of the room while the cooler air enters the room via the lower openings.

Hence, the correct option is (A).

73. Ascensional ventilation is when the airflow moves upwards through inclined workings. This takes advantage of the natural ventilation effects caused by the added heat to the air.

Hence, the correct option is (A).

74. Natural ventilation pressure assists the fan ventilation pressure in case of ascential ventilation.

Natural ventilation is the use of wind and thermal buoyancy to create air movement in and out of your home without the use of mechanical systems, with the goal of bringing fresh air into your home.

Ascensional ventilation is when the airflow moves upwards through inclined workings. This takes advantage of the natural ventilation effects caused by the added heat to the air.

Hence, the correct option is (A).

75. When the air and mineral flow in the same direction the ventilation is called Homotropal ventilation.

Two basic types of ventilation systems include homotropal and antitropial systems. Homotropal systems allow for the airflow within the mine to be transported in the same direction as the fresh air whereas antitropal systems remove contaminated air in the opposite direction of fresh air entering the mine.

Hence, the correct option is (C).

76. The effect of splitting the air in parallel decreases the overall resistence experienced by air in mines. This tends the flow towards the laminar and laminar layers have less resistence in between them.

Hence, the correct option is (B).

77. Air is used to carry ash in the pneumatic ash handling system.

In a pneumatic ash handling system, Air is used to carry ash to long-distance at a capacity of 5 to 30 tonnes per hour. The air used for this purpose is easily cleanable and can be exhausted back into the atmosphere after the complete filtration processes.

Hence, the correct option is (C).

78. The Pneumatic ash handling system is a noisy ash handling system.

The air is made to pass at very high pressure in order to carry out the ash for long-distance. Since the air is moving at high speed at high velocity in the conveying pipes, it tends to create a lot of noise by hitting the walls of the pipe at swift turns and curves.

Hence, the correct option is (C).

79. Water is used to carry ash in the hydraulic system.

Water is used as the medium to carry ash at high velocity. Depending on water pressure the system is divided into the low-pressure system and the High-pressure system. In the low-pressure system, sloped sumps are used to move the ash at low velocity, and in the high-pressure system, nozzle sprays used to ram up the speed of ash flow.

Hence, the correct option is (B).

80. Self-rescuer reviving apparatus used to administer pure oxygen to an unconscious person or affected by noxious gasses.

A Reviving apparatus is used to administrate to:

(1) An unconscious person,

(2) Whose breathing is considerably feeble for some other cause.

The treatment is given to the patient by the rescue team at a zone free from noxious gasses or at the fresh airbase.

Hence, the correct option is (B).

81. Loads are usually classified into unit load and bulk load. Solids form the majority of materials that are handled in the industrial situation. Solids are classified into two main groups: Unit load and Bulk load (materials).

Unit loads are those which are counted by numbers or units. A component of a machine, a complete machine, a structural element, a beam, a girder, building block are some examples of the unit load.

Bulk Load: When the load is in the form of particles or lumps of Homogenous materials or powder-like materials, which can not be counted by numbers, it is called as Bulk load. Examples are Sand, Cement. Coal. Mineral, Stone, Clay etc.

Hence, the correct option is (B).

82. Hosting equipment are usually powered equipment used for lifting and lowering unit and varying loads intermittently. The primary function of hoisting equipment is transferring through lifting and lowering operations.

The Hoisting drum of a crane is made of: Grey cast iron: grade 25 of IS: 210-1962 Cast steel: grade 2 of IS: 1030-1963 Mild steel IS:226-1962.

Hence, the correct option is (D).

83. Bulk loads are single rigid mass.

Bulk Load: When the load is in the form of particles or lumps of Homogenous materials or powder-like materials, which can not be counted by numbers, it is called as Bulk load. Examples are Sand, Cement. Coal. Mineral, Stone, Clay etc.

Hence, the correct option is (B).

84. Rope reeving is used to indicate the payload is lifted on two, four, or six or eight parts of the rope.

The purpose of a wire rope reeving system is to provide a mechanical advantage so the system can hoist heavy loads by applying relatively little force to the rope. The mechanical advantage equals the number of sections of wire rope actually supporting the load.

Hence, the correct option is (C).

85. Wherever the material is loaded onto a conveyor belt, impact idlers are installed beneath the troughed belt over the full loading length. Impact idlers sets are spaced at intervals of typically 350 mm to 450 mm in order to provide a comprehensive support base for the belt.

Hence, the correct option is (D).

86. Ash is abrasive as well as dusty. A Drag chain conveyor will be preferred for its handling.

The principle operation of a drag conveyor is based on material movement using a skeletal chain and flight assembly that is drawn along the bottom section of an enclosed housing. Slower chain speed means less wear, and less horsepower equals lower energy requirements and operating costs.

Hence, the correct option is (C).

87. Based on air pressures, pneumatic conveying systems may be classified as Positive pressure, negative pressure, combined positive-negative system.

- Positive pressure system: A positive low-pressure pipeline system is one in which a positive airflow, created by a positive displacement blower, effectively transports slow-flowing materials over a distance up to 500 meters.
- Negative pressure (or suction) system: In this type of conveyor, a positive displacement blower creates a vacuum in the conveyor pipeline, which causes the material to be sucked through one or multiple nozzles and conveyed to a receiving hopper.
- Combined negative-positive pressure (or combination) system: In this system, the principles of both the positive pressure system and suction system are employed. This type of pneumatic conveyor is particularly employed when materials from more than one point have to be picked up and simultaneously delivered to multiple delivery points.

Hence, the correct option is (C).

88. Selection of pneumatic handling system depends on properties of materials like bulk density, particle size, material characteristics like moisture content, abrasiveness, corrosiveness, fragility etc.

Hence, the correct option is (D).

89. Lay of steel wire ropes classifies into:

1. Regular Lay,

2. Lang's Lay,

3. Reverse Lay

The lay of a wire rope describes the manner in which either the wires in a strand or the strands in the rope, are laid in a helix.

Hence, the correct option is (A).

90. The selection of a particular type of pump depends on the capacity of the pump, the number of pump units, suction and discharge condition, type of drive, initial and final cost, lift, the flexibility of operations and floor space requirements.

Hence, the correct option is (A).

91. The speed at which the centrifugal pump runs lies in the range of 500 to 100 rotations per minute (r.p.m). Centrifugal pump impellers have specific speed values ranging from 500 to 10,000 rpm, radial flow pumps at 500-4000 rpm, mixed flow at 2000-8000 rpm, axial flow pumps at 7000-20,000 rpm.

Hence, the correct option is (C).

92. The centrifugal pump converts mechanical energy into hydraulic energy (flow, velocity, and pressure) and the AC motor converts electrical energy into mechanical energy.
Many medium and larger centrifugal pumps offer efficiencies of 75% to 93% and even the smaller ones usually fall into the 50% to 70% range.

Hence, the correct option is (C).

93. Method of correlates involves reducing the arithmetic work. It includes determination of the corrections for wavelength and their weights which help in establishing a network of information.

Hence, the correct option is (D).

94. Clients use SLP (Service Location Protocol) protocol to discover SMI Agents on the Storage Area Network.

The Service Location Protocol (SLP, srvloc) is a service discovery protocol that allows computers and other devices to find services in a local area network without prior configuration.

Hence, the correct option is (A).

95. The centrifugal pump has a continuous flow. It does not give a constant discharge under the variable head.

Centrifugal pumps are used to transport fluids by the conversion of rotational kinetic energy to the hydrodynamic energy of the fluid flow. The rotational energy typically comes from an engine or electric motor. They are a sub-class of dynamic axisymmetric work-absorbing turbomachinery. The fluid enters the pump impeller along or near to the rotating axis and is accelerated by the impeller, flowing radially outward into a diffuser or volute chamber (casing), from which it exits.

Hence, the correct option is (C).

96. Bill of the material structure is used to set requirements.

A bill of materials or product structure (sometimes bill of material, BOM, or associated list) is a list of the raw materials, sub-assemblies, intermediate assemblies, sub-components, parts, and the quantities of each needed to manufacture an end product.

Hence, the correct option is (A).

97. Just in time (JIT) inventory refers to an inventory management system with objectives of having inventory readily available to meet demand, but not to a point of excess where you must stockpile extra products. JIT inventory is used to help keep the cost down, free up physical space and reduce defect rates.

Hence, the correct option is (D).

98. Forecasting is used for Independent demand items.

Forecasting is a technique that uses historical data as inputs to make informed estimates that are predictive in determining the direction of future trends.

An inventory of an item is said to be falling into the category of independent demand when the demand for such an item is not dependant upon the demand for another item. Finished goods Items, which are ordered by External Customers or manufactured for stock and sale, are called independent demand items.

Hence, the correct option is (B).

99. Capacity Requirement Planning (CRP). The manufacturing order planned through the material planning (MRP or parts explosion) is usually submitted to the administration division or the person in charge of administration that comprehensively controls the manufacturing division, and the validity of its capacity and load is first determined.

The manufacturing order is created for each item using a bill of material based on the production schedule through the material planning, and thus at this point, the concept of process is not existing yet.

But items are actually produced through a number of processes. Capacity Requirements Planning refers to the planning where the load for each process is grasped according to the manufacturing order, the adjustments are made, and then the work of each process is planned.

It is necessary to set the capacity after considering the current situation, in order to make Capacity Requirements Planning more practical.

Hence, the correct option is (D).

100. Capacity planning is the process of determining the production capacity needed by an organization to meet changing demands for its products. In the context of capacity planning, design capacity is the maximum amount of work that an organization is capable of completing in a given period.

Hence, the correct option is (D).

Mock Test 05

General knowledge And Current Affairs

Q.1 In which of the following fields, the Nobel Prize, 2018 has not been announced?

[Super TET Paper - I, 2019]

A. Medical **B.** Literature
C. Physics **D.** Chemistry

Q.2 Under Akbar, the Mir Bakshi was required to look after:

A. Military affairs
B. The state treasury
C. The royal household
D. The land revenue system

Q.3 Which of the following has a potential for the harnessing of tidal energy in India?

A. Gulf of Cambay
B. Gulf of Mannar
C. Backwaters of Kerala
D. Chilika lake

Q.4 Police Officer Poonam Khatri crowned Wushu World Champion in which category?

A. 60 kg **B.** 70 kg **C.** 75 kg **D.** 85 kg

Q.5 NASA & ESA launched sentinel-6 Michael Freilich satellite by which launcher vehicle?

A. Falcon 9 rocket **B.** Cartosat-2
C. Atlas **D.** Ariane-5

Q.6 India and the European Union (EU) exchanged Note Verbale to renew its Agreement on Scientific and Technological Cooperation for how many years?

A. 4 **B.** 6 **C.** 5 **D.** 9

Q.7 Under which Article of the Constitution of India the President has the power of pardon or remission?

A. Article 72 **B.** Article 71
C. Article 76 **D.** Article 74

Q.8 The members of the State Public Service Commission are appointed by the:

A. Chief minister **B.** Chief justice
C. Governor **D.** Vice-president

Q.9 In which decade was the AIEE (now the IEEE) founded?

A. 1850s **B.** 1880s **C.** 1930s **D.** 1950s

Q.10 Resurgent India Bonds were issued in US dollar, Pound Sterling and:

A. Japanese Yen **B.** Deutsche Mark
C. Euro **D.** French Franc

Mine management, Legislation and General Safety

Q.11 What are the roles of HRD professionals?

(i) Planning
(ii) Staffing
(iii) Employee Development
(iv) Performance Management
(v) Employee Rewards
(vi) Maintaining the quality of Work-Life & Discipline

A. i, ii, iii, iv **B.** ii, iii, iv, v
C. iii, iv, v, vi **D.** All of the above

Q.12 What are the objectives of HRM?

(i) Societal Objectives
(ii) Organisational Objectives
(iii) Functional Objectives
(iv) Personal Objectives
(v) Statistical Objectives

A. i, ii, iii, iv **B.** ii, iii, iv, v
C. i, ii, iv, v **D.** All of the above

Q.13 HRM refers to:

A. A management function that helps managers to attract, set expectations & develop members for an organization
B. A set of programs, functions & activities designed & carried out for maximum efficiency
C. Both (A) and (B)
D. None of the above

Q.14 How can a good employment brand help HR?

(i) Keep ahead in the talent war.
(ii) Attract & induce the right kind of people she is looking for.
(iii) Enhance her ability to get quality resumes to choose from.
(iv) Retain her existing employee pool.
(v) Subsequently see a dip in employee turnover.

A. i, ii, iii, iv **B.** i, ii, iii, iv, v
C. i, ii, iv, v **D.** None of the above

Q.15 Individual Training needs are identified by:

(i) Performance Appraisals
(ii) Interviews
(iii) Questionnaires
(iv) Employee Engagement surveys
(v) Training Feedback

A. i, ii, iii, iv **B.** Only iii
C. i, ii, iv, v **D.** Both (B) and (C)

Q.16 Job Rotation can be defined as:

A. Lateral transfer of employees among a number of different positions and tasks within jobs which requires different skills and responsibilities

B. It helps to understand the different steps into creating a product or delivery

C. It permits individuals to gain experience in various phases of the business

D. All of the above

Q.17 Training & Development together helps in:

(i) Removing performance deficiencies.

(ii) Offer Greater stability.

(iii) Flexibility & capacity for growth.

(iv) Reduces accidents, wastages & damages to machinery.

(v) Reduces dissatisfaction, absenteeism & complaints.

A. i, ii, iii **B.** ii, iii, iv

C. i, ii, iii, iv, v **D.** None of the above

Q.18 Which organization theory can be understood by IF and THEN relationship?

A. System approach

B. Contingency approach

C. Process approach

D. Scientific approach

Q.19 Organization Behavior is:

A. An interdisciplinary approach

B. A humanistic approach

C. Total system approach

D. All of the above

Q.20 Organization Behavior is not a/an:

A. A separate field of study

B. Applied science

C. Normative science

D. Pessimistic approach

Q.21 "Cognitive theory" of learning was given by:

A. Skinner **B.** Pavlov **C.** Tolman **D.** Piaget

Q.22 Extension of behaviour modification into the organization is called:

A. Enrichment **B.** Enlargement

C. O.B. Modification **D.** O.B. External

Q.23 ___________is a relatively permanent change in behaviour that occurs as a result of experience.

A. Behaviour modification

B. Learning

C. Motivation

D. Skills

Q.24 The finance manager is accountable for:

A. Earning capital assets of the company

B. Effective management of a fund

C. Arrangement of financial resources

D. Proper utilization of funds

Q.25 From the below-mentioned items which are financial assets?

A. Machines **B.** Bonds

C. Stocks **D.** Both (B) and (C)

Q.26 The capital budget is associated with:

A. Long terms and short terms assets

B. Fixed assets

C. Long terms of assets

D. Short term assets

Q.27 Process improvement technique that sorts the "vital few" from the "trivial many" is:

A. Taguchi analysis **B.** Pareto analysis

C. Benchmarking **D.** Yamaguchi analysis

Q.28 A fishbone diagram is also known as a:

A. Cause-and-effect diagram

B. Poka-yoke diagram

C. Kaizen diagram

D. Taguchi diagram

Q.29 Which of the following functions is not a core function of an organisation?

A. The Product/Service Development Function

B. The Operations Function

C. The Marketing (Including Sales) Function

D. The accounting and finance function

Q.30 What is a perfect order?

A. Simultaneous achievement of relevant customer metrics

B. An order that arrives on time

C. An order that arrives undamaged

D. An order that is easy for the receiver to fill

Q.31 Total Quality Management emphasizes:

A. The responsibility of the Quality Control staff to identify and solve all quality-related problems

B. A commitment to quality that goes beyond internal company issues to suppliers and customers

C. A system where strong managers are the only decision-makers.

D. A process where mostly statisticians get involved

Q.32 What technique deals with the problem of supplying sufficient facilities to production lines or individuals that require uneven service?

A. Supply-demand theory

B. PERT

C. Inventory theory

D. Queuing theory

Q.33 Which of the following is not one of the major categories of costs associated with quality?

A. Prevention costs **B.** Appraisal costs

C. Internal failures **D.** None of the above

Q.34 According to the time estimates made by the PERT planners, the maximum time that would be needed to complete an activity is called ________.

A. The most likely time estimate

B. Optimistic time estimate

C. Pessimistic time estimate

D. Expected time estimate

Q.35 CPM was developed in which country?

A. Japan **B.** China **C.** USA **D.** Russia

Q.36 The performance of a specific task in CPM is known as a/an:

A. Dummy **B.** Event **C.** Activity **D.** Contract

Q.37 Concept of MBO (Management By Objectives) was introduced by:

A. Peter F. Drucker **B.** Mary Parker
C. Henri Fayol **D.** Philip Kotler

Q.38 Merit–Cum–Seniority is a method resorted to for:

A. Salary fixation **B.** Transfer
C. Promotion **D.** None of the above

Q.39 The full form of PLRS is:

A. Productivity Linked Reward Scheme
B. Performance Linked Reward Scheme
C. Parameter Loaded Reward Scheme
D. None of the above

Q.40 The following is minor penalty:

A. Demotion
B. Lowering stage of pay
C. Suspension
D. Withholding of increment

Winning and Working

Q.41 What is the colour of rose quartz attributed to?

A. Iron **B.** Titanium
C. Aluminium **D.** Sandstone

Q.42 The mineral not belonging to the quartz group is __________.

A. Amethyst **B.** Agate
C. Jasper **D.** Calcite

Q.43 The thickest coal seam is found in which of the following places of India?

A. Singrauli **B.** Jhingurda
C. Kargali **D.** Kamptee

Q.44 Gondwana coal is found in which of the following places of India?

1. Damodar valley
2. Mahanadi Valley
3. Raniganj
4. Singrauli

Choose the correct option from the codes given below:

A. 1 & 2 **B.** 1, 2 & 4
C. 2, 3 & 4 **D.** 1, 2, 3 & 4

Q.45 Which of the following operation is used to enlarge the previously drilled hole?

A. Reaming **B.** Tapping
C. Boring **D.** None of the above

Q.46 What does boring mean?

A. A process of making a hole in an object
B. A process of enlarging a hole in an object
C. A process of finishing an existing hole very smoothly and accurately in size
D. None of the above

Q.47 Boring is done with the help of a tool known as:

A. Taps **B.** Boring cutter
C. Cutting tool **D.** Twist drill

Q.48 What is the meaning of depillaring in reference to Coal-Mining?

A. Extraction of coal from the pillars formed during the process of development
B. Extraction of coal from the mines formed during the process of development
C. Extraction of coal from the ore formed during the process of development
D. None of the above

Q.49 Which mine machinery is used in Mechanized Long Wall Face?

A. Slider Support Mechanism
B. Powered Support Mechanism
C. Support Mechanism
D. None of the above

Q.50 Bord & Pillar Method carried out through how many operations?

A. By two operations—Development & Dipillaring
B. By three operations—Development, Dipillaring & Drawing
C. By one operations—Dipillaring
D. None of the above

Q.51 Gun-cotton is made by saturating cotton with______

A. Sulfonic acid **B.** Nitric acid
C. Sulphonic acid **D.** None of the above

Q.52 The dressing of stone is done:

A. Immediately after quarrying
B. After seasoning
C. After three months of quarrying
D. Just before the building

Q.53 The crushing strength of a stone depends upon its:

A. Texture **B.** Specific gravity
C. Workability **D.** Both (A) and (B)

Q.54 The money paid to the worker in cash without any additional advantages is called:

A. Nominal wages **B.** Real wages
C. Minimum wages **D.** Living wages

Q.55 What is the variation of total pressure with depth for any submerged surface if we neglect variation in the density?

A. Linear **B.** Parabolic
C. Curvilinear **D.** Logarithmic

Q.56 Which principle is used for calculating the centre of pressure?

A. Principle of momentum
B. Principle of conservation of energy
C. Principle of balancing of momentum
D. None of the above

Q.57 The instrument that is used to measure the relative humidity is:
A. Pitot tube **B.** Aneroid barometer
C. Hygrometer **D.** Anemometer

Q.58 A __________ device prevents the oscillation of the moving system and enables the latter to reach its final position quickly.
A. Deflecting **B.** Controlling
C. Damping **D.** All of the above

Q.59 What is the method of stoping for massive ore bodies of high-grade ore with walls mined out in a series or horizontal slices from the top of the ore body?
A. Top slicing **B.** Block caving
C. Square set stoping **D.** Sublevel stoping

Q.60 The depth of excavation of foundations is generally measured with a
A. Ranging Rod **B.** Steel tape
C. Leveling staff **D.** Bonning rod

Surface environment, Mine Ventilation and Hazards

Q.61 H_2 has an explosive limit:
A. 12.5 - 74% **B.** 5.4 - 14.8%
C. 4 - 45% **D.** 4 - 75%

Q.62 H_2S has an explosive limit?
A. 12.5 - 74% **B.** 5.4 - 14.8%
C. 4 - 45% **D.** 4 - 75%

Q.63 The permissible limit of White Damp is:
A. 5 ppm **B.** 7 ppm **C.** 10 ppm **D.** 50 ppm

Q.64 The shot firer shall carefully test for inflammable gas at all places within a radius of__ the place of firing.
A. 12 m **B.** 18 m **C.** 22 m **D.** 25 m

Q.65 Modern flame safety lamps can withstand an air velocity of:
A. 5 m/s **B.** 10 m/s **C.** 15 m/s **D.** 20 m/s

Q.66 Which force is involved in the Chromatography?
A. Hydrogen bonding **B.** London force
C. Electrostatic force **D.** All of the above

Q.67 Which of the following is the disadvantage of the coiled or helical shaped packed chromatographic column?
A. It cannot be packed uniformly
B. It cannot be repacked easily
C. It is not compact
D. It is not easy to heat it evenly

Q.68 Capillary columns are open tubular columns constructed from which of the following materials?
A. Glass **B.** Metal
C. Stainless steel **D.** Fused silica

Q.69 No road for trucks and dumper shall have a gradient steeper than at least____at any place.
A. 1 in 6 **B.** 1 in 7 **C.** 1 in 10 **D.** 1 in 14

Q.70 Upto what depth from the surface the temparature is constant?
A. 10m **B.** 15m **C.** 20m **D.** 25m

Q.71 Which system consumes less power out of all ash handling systems?
A. Mechanical ash handling system
B. Pneumatic ash handling system
C. Hydraulic ash handling system
D. Steam jet ash handling system

Q.72 What is the function of cyclone separators in pneumatic ash handling system?
A. To separate the lighter dust particles
B. To force up the movement of ash through pipes or tubes
C. To draw out the dust from furnace
D. To separate minute coal particles

Q.73 The best extinguisher for fires due to oil is:
A. CO_2 type **B.** Foam type
C. Water - CO_2 type **D.** Soda acid type

Q.74 The best extinguisher for gaseous fires is:
A. Dry powder **B.** CO_2 type
C. Foam type **D.** Water - CO_2 type

Q.75 The __________ alarm system consists of handbell or such other arrangement by which the occupants of the whole or part of the building are informed about the happening of a fire.
A. Man-made **B.** Manual
C. Automatic **D.** Electric

Q.76 ______________ include portable fire extinguishers, the usual being carbon dioxide type.
A. Manual fire extinguisher
B. Automatic sprinkler
C. Internal hydrants
D. Water taps

Q.77 ______________ arrangement consists of a system of overhead pipe which are fixed in the ceiling of the roof.
A. Fire extinguishers **B.** Internal hydrants
C. Automatic sprinkler **D.** Water pipes

Q.78 Swampy land is _______.
A. Ill-aerated land
B. The land where cultivation operations are impossible
C. Land having deposition of alkali salts in the root zone of the crops
D. Saline land

Q.79 Which of the following is a remedial measure for water-logging?

A. Controlling seepage from the canals
B. By lowering the F.S.L of the canals
C. Quick disposal of rainwater
D. Installation of lift irrigation systems

Q.80 Which of the following factor do not contribute to water-logging?

A. Inadequate drainage
B. Seepage from unlined canals
C. Frequent flooding
D. Excessive tapping of groundwater

Mine Machineries, surveying and electricity

Q.81 Which of the following is not characteristic of nylon rope?

A. Its strength is affected by drying oils, such as linseed oil
B. It is well suited to shock loading
C. It starts to burn at 300 Fahrenheit
D. It is highly resistant to mildew and rot

Q.82 The best general-purpose rope, especially for critical uses, is made from _________.

A. Polyethylene **B.** Polyester
C. Nylon **D.** Polypropylene

Q.83 P.R.U. pump dust sampler uses the principle of:

A. Thermal precipitation
B. Impaction
C. Impingement i.e inertia precipitation
D. Scattering of light

Q.84 The mostly used blade type in centrifugal fan is:

A. Backward **B.** Radial
C. Forward **D.** None of the above

Q.85 Konimeter dust sampler uses the principle of:

A. Thermal precipitation
B. Gravity
C. Impingement i.e. inertia precipitation
D. Optical method

Q.86 An industrial unit which offers its entire production for export.

A. EOU **B.** FTZ
C. EPZ **D.** Industrial estate

Q.87 Crater wear is predominant in

A. Carbon tool steels
B. Tungsten carbide tools
C. High-speed steel tools
D. Ceramic tools

Q.88 A triac is a:

A. 2 terminal switch
B. 2 terminal bilateral switch
C. 3 terminal bilateral switch
D. 3 terminal bidirectional switch

Q.89 The minimum duration of the pulse in a pulse triggering system for thyristors should be at :

A. 10 μs **B.** 10 ms **C.** 30 ms **D.** 1 sec

Q.90 For very high-speed ratio the indispensable drive is:

A. Direct drive **B.** Rope drive
C. Chain drive **D.** All of the above

Q.91 15 minute rated motors are suitable for:

A. Light duty cranes
B. Medium-duty cranes
C. Heavy-duty cranes
D. All of the above

Q.92 For medium-duty cranes the short time rating motor used is _____ .

A. 10 minutes **B.** 15 minutes
C. 30 minutes **D.** None of the above

Q.93 In order to avoid permanent sulfating of the plates in a lead-acid battery, the voltage of the lamp on usage must not be allowed to fall below:

A. 1.8 V per cell **B.** 2.2 V per cell
C. 4.4 V per cell **D.** 1.18 V per cell

Q.94 In electric lighting, the power cannot be used at a voltage exceeding:

A. 30 **B.** 110 **C.** 220 **D.** 250

Q.95 Static pressure is measured by?

A. Barometer **B.** Pitot tube
C. Venturi meter **D.** U-tube

Q.96 Velocity pressure is measured by:

A. Barometer **B.** Inclined manometer
C. U-tube **D.** Pitot tube

Q.97 MRP-II system is called a closed-loop system because it considers:

A. Inventory **B.** Finance
C. Manpower **D.** None of the above

Q.98 P.M.T.S(Predetermined Motion Time System) include:

A. M.T.M (Method Time Measurement)
B. W.F.S (Work Factor Systems)
C. B.M.T.S (Basic Motion Time Study)
D. All of the above

Q.99 The maximum working hours in a day is:

A. 6 hours **B.** 8 hours **C.** 9 hours **D.** 12 hours

Q.100 The method of stoping best suited to low-grade deposits of horizontal or mild dip and of thickness up to 5m is:

A. Open stoping **B.** Breast stoping
C. Sublevel stoping **D.** Shrinkage stoping

// Smart Answer Sheet //

Correct Percentage of students who answered correctly. **Skipped** Percentage of students who skipped.

Q.	Ans.	Correct	Skipped	Q.	Ans.	Correct	Skipped	Q.	Ans.	Correct	Skipped	Q.	Ans.	Correct	Skipped	Q.	Ans.	Correct	Skipped	Q.	Ans.	Correct	Skipped
1	B	65.64 %	1.44 %	18	B	83.43 %	0.0 %	35	C	77.42 %	0.0 %	52	A	41.92 %	1.6 %	69	D	31.35 %	3.6 %	86	C	40.93 %	1.32 %
2	A	44.92 %	1.8 %	19	D	82.23 %	0.0 %	36	C	87.2 %	0.0 %	53	D	89.34 %	0.0 %	70	B	88.09 %	0.0 %	87	B	45.52 %	1.8 %
3	A	49.93 %	1.69 %	20	D	68.15 %	1.1 %	37	A	68.77 %	1.37 %	54	A	66.97 %	1.09 %	71	A	62.16 %	1.92 %	88	D	78.48 %	0.0 %
4	C	89.0 %	0.0 %	21	D	89.51 %	0.0 %	38	C	66.56 %	1.08 %	55	A	53.4 %	1.97 %	72	A	68.61 %	1.02 %	89	A	17.35 %	3.02 %
5	A	55.25 %	1.52 %	22	C	65.73 %	1.89 %	39	A	87.39 %	0.0 %	56	C	85.19 %	0.0 %	73	B	83.94 %	0.0 %	90	B	58.79 %	1.77 %
6	C	67.53 %	1.15 %	23	B	77.71 %	0.0 %	40	D	84.44 %	0.0 %	57	C	78.66 %	0.0 %	74	A	63.86 %	1.02 %	91	A	85.33 %	0.0 %
7	A	85.41 %	0.0 %	24	C	45.97 %	1.89 %	41	B	80.43 %	0.0 %	58	C	69.16 %	1.61 %	75	B	66.07 %	1.15 %	92	C	67.44 %	1.96 %
8	C	77.95 %	0.0 %	25	D	87.66 %	0.0 %	42	D	64.95 %	1.6 %	59	A	69.57 %	1.06 %	76	A	84.52 %	0.0 %	93	A	58.89 %	1.77 %
9	B	41.36 %	1.13 %	26	C	63.94 %	1.91 %	43	B	68.68 %	1.7 %	60	D	60.55 %	1.13 %	77	C	78.72 %	0.0 %	94	D	60.06 %	1.37 %
10	B	84.74 %	0.0 %	27	B	62.58 %	1.81 %	44	D	65.92 %	1.63 %	61	D	14.03 %	4.29 %	78	B	87.46 %	0.0 %	95	D	69.56 %	1.65 %
11	D	14.57 %	3.69 %	28	A	46.54 %	1.34 %	45	C	88.34 %	0.0 %	62	C	17.5 %	4.04 %	79	D	77.37 %	0.0 %	96	D	80.88 %	0.0 %
12	A	66.77 %	1.05 %	29	A	78.89 %	0.0 %	46	B	85.59 %	0.0 %	63	D	66.68 %	1.05 %	80	D	76.79 %	0.0 %	97	B	53.98 %	1.55 %
13	C	51.64 %	1.78 %	30	A	45.73 %	1.79 %	47	B	80.08 %	0.0 %	64	B	55.39 %	1.93 %	81	C	82.53 %	0.0 %	98	D	54.1 %	1.16 %
14	B	54.58 %	1.35 %	31	B	60.06 %	1.61 %	48	A	59.91 %	1.37 %	65	C	44.55 %	1.84 %	82	B	46.25 %	1.79 %	99	C	77.75 %	0.0 %
15	D	80.57 %	0.0 %	32	D	51.12 %	1.54 %	49	B	61.53 %	1.05 %	66	D	53.81 %	1.82 %	83	D	69.1 %	1.2 %	100	B	58.34 %	1.59 %
16	D	59.24 %	1.86 %	33	D	41.64 %	1.02 %	50	A	10.88 %	3.79 %	67	B	45.91 %	1.99 %	84	A	87.96 %	0.0 %				
17	C	58.22 %	1.07 %	34	C	62.77 %	1.42 %	51	B	49.61 %	1.03 %	68	D	81.75 %	0.0 %	85	C	64.95 %	1.54 %				

//Hints and Solutions//

1. In the Literature field, the Nobel Prize, 2018 has not been announced.

The Swedish Academy has said no Nobel prize for literature will be awarded in 2018 year for the first time in 70 years because of a #MeToo scandal.

Polish novelist Olga Tokarczuk and Austrian author Peter Handke, two writers whose works are deeply intertwined in Europe's religious, ethnic, and social fault lines, won the 2018 and 2019 Nobel Prizes for literature respectively.

Hence, the correct option is (B).

2. The head of the military was called the Mir Bakshi, appointed from among the leading nobles of the court. The Mir Bakshi was in charge of intelligence gathering, and also made recommendations to the emperor for military appointments and promotions.

Hence, the correct option is (A).

3. Gulf of Cambay has potential for the harnessing of tidal energy in India.

Tidal energy is renewable energy powered by the natural rise and fall of ocean tides and currents. Some of these technologies include turbines and paddles.

According to the estimates of the Indian government, the country has a potential of 8,000 MW of tidal energy. This includes about 7,000 MW in the Gulf of Cambay in Gujarat, 1,200 MW in the Gulf of Kutch and 100 MW in the Gangetic delta in the Sunderbans region of West Bengal.

Hence, the correct option is (A).

4. Indian Police Officer, Poonam Khatri has claimed World Championship status after her silver medal at the Wushu World Championship last year has been upgraded to a Gold medal. Poonam hails from Haryana's Jhajjar district. Poonam had lost the final to Iranian opponent Mariyam in the Women's 75 kg category but after Mariyam recently failed the dope test, the gold medal has been awarded to Poonam Khatri. The information was clarified by Secretary-General of the Indian Wushu Association, Suhel Ahmed.

Hence, the correct option is (C).

5. NASA & ESA launched sentinel-6 Michael Freilich satellite by SpaceX Falcon 9 rocket from California. Sentinel-6 Michael Freilich, the latest in a series of spacecraft designed to monitor our oceans, is scheduled to launch from Vandenberg Air Force Base in central California on November 21, 2020.

Hence, the correct option is (A).

6. India and European Union (EU) exchanged Note Verbale to renew its Agreement on Scientific and Technological Cooperation for the next five years (2020-2025) which expired on May 17, 2020. It was initially inked on 23 November 2001 and renewed two times in the past in 2007 and 2015. This renewal is on the lines of the decision taken by both nations during the virtual 15th India-EU Summit which was led by Prime Minister Narendra Modi from India's side.

Hence, the correct option is (C).

7. The President shall have the power to grant pardons, reprieves or remissions of punishment or to suspend, remit or commute the sentence of any person convicted of any offence under Article 72 of the Constitution of India.

Hence, the correct option is (A).

8. A State Public Service Commission (SPSC) comprises a chairman and other members appointed by the governor of the state. One-half of the appointed members of the commission should have held office for at least ten years either under the government of India or under the government of a state.

Hence, the correct option is (C).

9. In the 1880s decade, AIEE (now IEEE) was founded.

The American Institute of Electrical Engineers (AIEE) was a United States-based organization of electrical engineers which was founded in 1884, that existed from 1884 through 1962. On January 1, 1963, it merged with the Institute of Radio Engineers (IRE) to form the Institute of Electrical and Electronics Engineers (IEEE).

Hence, the correct option is (B).

10. The Resurgent India Bonds (RIBs) are bank instruments issued by SBI representing foreign currency denominated deposits in the form of promissory notes. Offered to Non-Resident Indians and Overseas Corporate Bodies. Bonds being denominated in foreign currency i.e., in US dollar, Pound Sterling and Deutsche Mark. Bonds are free from forex risk. State Bank of India has announced the scheme, effective from 5th August 1998.

Hence, the correct option is (B).

11. At present, the HRD Professionals acts as a strategic adviser to help the decision-makers on issues related to HRD. They also play the role of an HR systems designer and developer by assisting the HR management in designing and developing HR systems in an organization to increase its performance. They also act as organizational change agents by helping the management in designing and implementing change strategies to transform the organization. The result is more efficient work teams, intervention strategies, quality management and change reports.

Hence, the correct option is (D).

12. The primary objective of HRM is to ensure the availability of a competent and willing workforce for an organization. Beyond this, there are other objectives too. Specifically, HRM objectives are fourfold: Societal, Organizational, Functional and personal.

Personal Objectives: To assist Employees in achieving their personal goals, at least in so far as these goals enhance the individual's contribution to the organization.

Functional Objectives: To maintain the contribution of the department at an appropriate level organization should fulfill the needs.

Organizational Objectives: To recognize the role of HRM in bringing about organizational effectiveness.

Societal Objectives: To be ethically & socially responsible for the needs and challenges of society.

Hence, the correct option is (A).

13. Human resource management (HRM) is the practice of recruiting, hiring, deploying and managing an organization's employees. HRM is often referred to simply as human resources (HR). It primarily refers to handling employees and acknowledging their requirements for maintaining a positive work culture. The objective of HRM is to ensure a stable work environment with data in one place and efficient operations.

Hence, the correct option is (C).

14. Human resource management (HRM or HR) is the strategic approach to the effective management of people in a company or organization such that they help their business gain a competitive advantage. It is designed to maximize employee performance in the service of an employer's strategic objectives. A positive employment brand communicates that the organization is a good employer and a great place to work. Employer brand affects the recruitment of new employees, retention and engagement of current employees, and the overall perception of the organization in the market.

Hence, the correct option is (B).

15. Training needs analysis is a process by which an organisation defines the training needs that are required for individuals, a group, team, department or industry sector. The focus is on the job role of those involved and what skills and knowledge are needed in order to perform that job competently.

The Top 10 training needs of today's employees are:

1. Leadership development,

2. Interpersonal skills training,

3. Communication skills training,

4. Managing change,

5. Teamwork,

6. Management skills training,

7. Problem-solving,

8. Customer service,

9. Retaining employees,

10. Creativity and innovation.

Hence, the correct option is (D).

16. Job rotation is the practice of moving employees between jobs in an organization. These rotations are predominantly lateral, meaning that they happen between jobs on the same level and are not considered promotions. They are also often temporary with people moving back to their original job after a certain time.

As a multidisciplinary field, organizational behavior has been influenced by developments in a number of allied disciplines including sociology, psychology, economics, and engineering as well as by the experience of practitioners.

Hence, the correct option is (D).

17. The benefits and value of training and development activities as a domino effect. leaders feel competent and can efficiently influence employee performance, happy and skilled workers create job satisfaction, commitment and thus retention; workforce improvement and engagement impacts the overall profit.

Hence, the correct option is (C).

18. The contingency approach refers to the idea that business leaders need to adjust leadership styles based on the situation at hand. It becomes a balance of a business leader's natural style and understanding when and where it needs to be altered.

Hence, the correct option is (B).

19. Organizational behaviour is the study of how people behave within groups. Early studies determined the importance of group dynamics in business productivity. The study of organizational behaviour is a foundation of corporate human resources.

As a multidisciplinary field, organizational behavior has been influenced by developments in a number of allied disciplines including sociology, psychology, economics, and engineering as well as by the experience of practitioners.

Hence, the correct option is (D).

20. Pessimistic describes the state of mind of someone who always expects the worst. A pessimistic attitude isn't very hopeful, shows little optimism, and can be a downer for everyone else. Hence, the pessimistic approach is not an organizational behavior.

Hence, the correct option is (D).

21. Cognitive theory is an approach to psychology that attempts to explain human behaviour by understanding your thought processes. For example, a therapist is using principles of cognitive theory when they teach you how to identify maladaptive thought patterns and transform them into constructive ones.

Piaget's stage theory describes the cognitive development of children. Cognitive development involves changes in the cognitive process and abilities.

In Piaget's view, early cognitive development involves processes based upon actions and later progresses to changes in mental operations.

Hence, the correct option is (D).

22. The Extension of behaviour modification into the organization is called Organisational Behaviour Modification (O.B. Mod.).

With its roots in modern behaviourist psychology, O.B. Mod. is a human resources management technique aimed at improving job-related behaviours that are observable and measurable, such as absenteeism or tardiness, or toward behaviour products, such as quality or quantity of work.

Hence, the correct option is (C).

23. Learning is defined as a relatively permanent change in behavior that occurs as a result of experience. Demonstrates some depth and breadth of understanding about operant conditioning theory. Operant conditioning refers to learning that involves rewards or punishments which come after a behavior.

Hence, the correct option is (B).

24. The finance manager is accountable for the arrangement of financial resources.

A Finance Manager distributes the financial resources of a company, is responsible for the budget planning, and supports the executive management team by offering insights and financial advice that will allow them to make the best business decisions for the company.

The financial manager's responsibilities include

• financial planning

• investing (spending money)

• and financing (raising money)

• Maximizing the value of the firm is the main goal of the financial manager, whose decisions often have long-term effects.

Hence, the correct option is (C).

25. A financial asset is a liquid asset that gets its value from a contractual right or ownership claim. Cash, stocks, bonds, mutual funds, and bank deposits are all are examples of financial assets. Unlike land, property, commodities, or other tangible physical assets, financial assets do not necessarily have inherent physical worth or even a physical form. Rather, their value reflects factors of supply and demand in the marketplace in which they trade, as well as the degree of risk they carry.

Hence, the correct option is (D).

26. The capital budget is associated with long terms of assets.

Capital budgeting or investment appraisal is the planning process used to determine whether an organization's long term investments such as new machinery, replacement of machinery, new plants, new products, and research development projects are worth the funding of cash through the firm's capitalization structure (debt, equity or retained earnings).

Hence, the correct option is (C).

27. The Process improvement technique that sorts the "vital few" from the "trivial many" is Pareto analysis.

Pareto Analysis is a statistical technique in decision-making used for the selection of a limited number of tasks that produce a significant overall effect. It uses the Pareto Principle (also known as the 80/20 rule) the idea that by doing 20% of the work you can generate 80% of the benefit of doing the entire job.

Hence, the correct option is (B).

28. The fishbone diagram or Ishikawa diagram is a cause-and-effect diagram that helps managers to track down the reasons for imperfections, variations, defects, or failures. The diagram looks just like a fish's skeleton with the problem at its head and the causes for the problem feeding into the spine.

Hence, the correct option is (A).

29. The Product/Service Development Function is not a core function of an organisation. The three major business functions are finance, marketing and operations. New product development (NPD) is a process of taking a product or service from conception to market. The process sets out a series of stages that new products typically go through, beginning with ideation and concept generation, and ending with the product's introduction to the market.

Hence, the correct option is (A).

30. Simultaneous achievement of relevant customer metrics is considered as a perfect order.

Customer metrics represent more than just numerical scores. Customer metrics have a deeper meaning, representing some underlying characteristic/mental processes about your customers: their opinions and attitudes about and intentions toward your company or brand.

Hence, the correct option is (A).

31. Total quality management (TQM) is a structured approach to overall organizational management. The focus of the process is to improve the quality of an organization's outputs, including goods and services, through the continual improvement of internal practices.

The 8 universal principles of quality management are:

1. Customer focus
2. Leadership
3. People involvement
4. Process approach
5. Systematic approach to management
6. Continual improvement
7. Factual approach to decision making
8. Mutually beneficial supplier relations

Hence, the correct option is (B).

32. Queuing theory deals with the problem of supplying sufficient facilities to production lines or individuals that require uneven service.

Any queuing activity can be summarized as entities (customers in the supermarket queue, or jobs in a computer queue) trying to get through an activity (waiting to be served). Queues happen when we can't all access the activity at the same time. when it is not economically efficient to have enough checkout lines for everyone to go right through as soon as they were ready, or there isn't enough server space to do an unlimited amount of computer tasks at one moment. Queuing theory deals with problems that involve queuing (or waiting). Typical examples might be:

- Banks/supermarkets - waiting for service,
- Computers - waiting for a response,

- Failure situations - waiting for a failure to occur e.g. in a piece of machinery,
- Public transport - waiting for a train or a bus.

Hence, the correct option is (D).

33. Quality costs are the costs associated with preventing, detecting, and remediating product issues related to quality. Quality costs do not involve simply upgrading the perceived value of a product to a higher standard. Instead, quality involves creating and delivering a product that meets the expectations of a customer. The Cost of Quality can be divided into four categories. They include Prevention costs, Appraisal costs, Internal Failure and External Failure.

Hence, the correct option is (D).

34. According to the time estimates made by the PERT planners, the maximum time that would be needed to complete an activity is called the pessimistic time estimate. This estimate does not include possible effects of floods, earthquakes, etc.

Hence, the correct option is (C).

35. CPM was developed in the United States of America(USA). The critical path method (CPM) is a project modeling technique developed in the late 1950s by Morgan R. Walker of DuPont and James E. Kelley Jr. of Remington Rand. Kelley attributed the term "critical path" to the developers of the PERT which was developed at about the same time by Booz Allen Hamilton and the U.S. Navy.

Hence, the correct option is (C).

36. The performance of a specific task in CPM is known as an activity.

Any individual operation, which utilizes resources and has a beginning and an end is called an activity. An arrow is used to depict an activity with its head indicating the direction of progress in the project. Critical path activities are the project tasks that must start and finish on time to ensure that the project ends on schedule. A delay in any critical path activity will delay the completion of the project unless the project plan can be adjusted so that successor tasks finish more quickly than planned.

Hence, the correct option is (C).

37. • The Concept of MBO (Management by objectives) was introduced by Peter F. Drucker in the 1950s.

• Management by objectives (MBO) is a strategic management model that aims to improve organizational performance by clearly defining objectives that are agreed to by both management and employees.

• According to the theory, having a say in goal setting and action plans encourages participation and commitment among employees, as well as aligning objectives across the organization.

Hence, the correct option is (A).

38. Merit–Cum–Seniority is a method resorted to for Promotion. The principle of Merit-cum-Seniority puts greater emphasis on merit and ability and where promotion is governed by this principle seniority plays a less significant role. However, seniority is to be given weightage when merit and ability more or less are equal among the candidates who are to be promoted.

Hence, the correct option is (C).

39. The full form of PLRS is the "Productivity Linked Reward Scheme".

The scheme of Productivity Linked Reward (PLR) for the employees/workers of Major Port Trusts and Dock Labour Board, wherein Productivity Linked Reward is granted on the basis of the composite Ports Performance Index (50% weightage to All India Performance and 50% weightage to individual port).

Hence, the correct option is (A).

40. Minor Penalties is defined as the reduction to a lower stage in the time-scale of pay by one stage for a period not exceeding three years, without cumulative effect and not adversely affecting his pension. Hence, "Withholding of increments of pay" is a type of minor penalty.

Hence, the correct option is (D).

41. Rose quartz is a special type of quartz and is known for its distinct rose-red colour. The colour is attributed to the presence of titanium.

Hence, the correct option is (B).

42. The mineral not belonging to the quartz group is Calcite. Amethyst quartz, agate and jasper belong to the quartz group, whereas, calcite belongs to the carbonate group whose chemical composition is completely different compared to the quartz group.

Hence, the correct option is (D).

43. The thickest coal seam is found in Jhingurda, Madhya Pradesh. The calorific value of the coal varies from 4,200-5,900 Kcal/kg.

Almost all of India's coal reserves are of Gondwana coal. The thickness of coal seams in Indian coalfields generally ranges from 1m to 30m.

Hence, the correct option is (B).

44. Gondwana coal makes up to 98 percent of the total reserves and 99 percent of the production of coal in India. Some name of places of Gondwana coals are the following:

The Damodar Valley Coalfield: It is the largest coalfield in India that extended to Jharkhand and West Bengal.

The Mahanadi Coalfield: It is located in Chhattisgarh and Odisha. Korba district, Vishrampur, Jhilmil and Chirmir (Ambikapur district) in Chhattisgarh; Talcher (Dhenkanal district) and Rampur-Hingir (Sambalpur) in Odisha are major mining fields.

Raniganj Coalfield: It is spread across the Indian states of West Bengal and Jharkhand. That makes it the second-largest coalfield in the country.

Singrauli Coalfield: Singrauli Coalfield is spread across the districts of Singrauli and Sonebhadra in the Indian states of Madhya Pradesh and Uttar Pradesh, mostly in the basin of the Son River.

Almost all of India's coal reserves are of Gondwana coal.

Hence, the correct option is (D).

45. The tool, which is used to enlarge a previously drilled hole is known as Boring tool.

Boring is a machining process for enlarging or finishing of an existing hole. When fine boring achieving an excellent surface finish and close tolerances are the main goal. Reaming is a finishing operation performed with a multi-edge tool giving high-precision holes with great surface finish, superb hole quality and close dimensional tolerances.

Hence, the correct option is (C).

46. Boring is a machining process for enlarging or finishing of an existing hole. When fine boring. achieving an excellent surface finish and close tolerances are the main goal. Reaming is a finishing operation performed.

Hence, the correct option is (B).

47. Boring is done with the help of a tool known as a boring cutter.

A Boring cutter is a device for producing smooth and accurate holes in a workpiece by enlarging existing holes with a bore, which may bear a single cutting tip of steel, cemented carbide, or diamond may be a small grinding wheel.

Hence, the correct option is (B).

48. Depillaring is the process of extraction of coal from pillars. It is also called pillar cutting or broken working.

In a method of depillaring, known as the caving method, the coal of the pillars is extracted and the roof is allowed to break and collapse into the voids or the decoaled area, known as goaf. As the roof strata about the coal seam break, the ground surface develops cracks and subsides, the extent of damage depending upon depth, thickness of the seam extracted, the nature of strata, thickness of the subsoil and effect of drag by faults.

Hence, the correct option is (A).

49. Powered Support Mechanism is used in Mechanized Long Wall Face.

The function of the powered supports are to:

• To control strata deformation, fracture and movement around the coal face,

• To maintain a safe and coal-producing working environment,

• To limit the amount of roof to floor convergence,

• To prevent broken rock from entering the work area, and

• To secure and advance all plants on the coal face including the roof supports.

Hence, the correct option is (B).

50. Bord & Pillar Method carried out through two operations - Development & Dipillaring.

The Board and Pillar method of mining coal seams involves the driving of a series of narrow headings in the seam parallel to each other and connected by cross headings so as to form pillars for subsequent extraction, either partial or complete, as geological conditions or necessity for supporting the surface, may permit.

Ideally, the pillars should be square but they are sometimes rectangular or of rhombus shape and the galleries surrounding the pillars are invariable of square cross-section. The bord and pillar method of mining is suited to work flat coal seams of average thickness and at shallow depths. Coal seams of 1.8 to 3 m thickness are best suited for this method, though the method has been successful in thinner seams also down to a thickness of 1.2 m and in thicker seams up to 4.8 m in thickness.

Hence, the correct option is (A).

51. Gun-cotton is made by saturating cotton with nitric acid.

Gun-cotton is defined as nitrocellulose also known as trinitrocellulose and cellulose nitrate is a mild explosive.

It is used in rockets, propellants, printing ink bases, leather finishing, and celluloid.

Hence, the correct option is (B).

52. The dressing of stone is done immediately after quarrying.

Quarrying is the process of removing rock, sand, gravel or other minerals from the ground in order to use them to produce materials for construction or other uses.

Dressing of Stone is the working of quarried stone into the shape and size required for use. This can be necessary as stones obtained from quarrying generally do not have the exact required dimensions or finish.

Hence, the correct option is (A).

53. The crushing strength of a stone depends upon its texture and specific gravity.

Crushing strength or compressive strength of a stone is the load per unit area at which the stone starts cracking. It should be greater than 100 N/mm^2 to ensure sufficient strength for use in construction.

Hence, the correct option is (D).

54. The money paid to the worker in cash without any additional advantages is called Nominal wages.

Nominal wages are the wages received by a worker in the form of money. On the other hand, real wages can be defined as the number of goods and services that a worker purchases from his/her nominal wages.

Hence, the correct option is (A).

55. The total pressure is given by $F=W\times A\times Y$

Where,

F=Force,

W=Specific weight,

A=Area.

Y=distance of central pressure from the surface of water/fluid.

Hence, F ∝ Y i.e linear relation.

Hence, the correct option is (A).

56. The Principle of balancing momentum is used for calculating the centre of pressure.

The center of pressure is the point where the total sum of a pressure field acts on a body, causing a force to act through that point. The total force vector acting at the center of pressure is the value of the integrated vectorial pressure field. We balance the moment in order to calculate the position of the centre of pressure.

Hence, the correct option is (C).

57. The instrument that is used to measure the relative humidity is a hygrometer.

Relative humidity tells us how much water vapour is in the air, compared to how much it could hold at that temperature. For example, Relative humidity of 50 percent means the air is holding one half of the water vapour it can hold.

Hence, the correct option is (C).

58. A damping device prevents the oscillation of the moving system and enables the latter to reach its final position quickly.

Damping is an effect that reduces the amplitude of oscillations in an oscillatory system, particularly the harmonic oscillator. This effect is linearly related to the velocity of the oscillations. This device uses the viscous drag of a fluid, such as oil, to provide a resistance that is related linearly to velocity.

Hence, the correct option is (C).

59. The method of stoping for massive ore bodies of high-grade ore with walls mined out in a series of horizontal slices from the top of the ore body is called top-slicing.

Stoping is the process of extracting the desired ore or other minerals from an underground mine, leaving behind an open space known as a stope. Stoping is used when the country rock is sufficiently strong not to collapse into the stope, although in most cases artificial support is also provided.

Hence, the correct option is (A).

60. The depth of excavation of foundations is generally measured with a Bonning rod.

Boning rods are used to set out horizontal lines or lines with a constant slope. In particular, they are used for setting out canal excavation works, but also for roads and dyke construction. Dykes are embankments constructed of earth or other suitable materials to protect land against overflow or flooding from streams, lakes, and tidal influences, and also to protect flat land from diffused surface waters.

Hence, the correct option is (D).

61. Before a fire or explosion can occur, three conditions must be met simultaneously.

A fuel (i.e. combustible gas) and oxygen (air) must exist in certain proportions, along with an ignition source, such as a spark or flame. The ratio of fuel and oxygen that is required varies with each combustible gas or vapour. The minimum concentration of a particular combustible gas or vapour necessary to support its combustion in air is defined as the Lower Explosive Limit (LEL) for that gas. Below this level, the mixture is too "lean" to burn. The maximum concentration of a gas or vapour that will burn in the air is defined as the Upper Explosive Limit (UEL). Above this level, the mixture is too "rich" to burn. The range between the LEL and UEL is known as the flammable range for that gas or vapour.

The explosive limits based on the volume percent of hydrogen in air at 14.7 psia (1 atm, 101 kPa) are 4.0 (Lower Explosive Limit) and 75.0 (Upper Explosive Limit).

Hence, the correct option is (D).

62. Before a fire or explosion can occur, three conditions must be met simultaneously.

A fuel (i.e. combustible gas) and oxygen (air) must exist in certain proportions, along with an ignition source, such as a spark or flame. The ratio of fuel and oxygen that is required varies with each combustible gas or vapour. The minimum concentration of a particular combustible gas or vapour necessary to support its combustion in air is defined as the Lower Explosive Limit (LEL) for that gas. Below this level, the mixture is too "lean" to burn. The maximum concentration of a gas or vapour that will burn in the air is defined as the Upper Explosive Limit (UEL). Above this level, the mixture is too "rich" to burn. The range between the LEL and UEL is known as the flammable range for that gas or vapour.

The explosive limits based on the volume percent of hydrogen sulfide in the air at atmospheric pressure are 4.0 (Lower Explosive Limit) and 44.0 (Upper Explosive Limit).

Hence, the correct option is (C).

63. The permissible limit of White Damp is 50 ppm.

White damp is a poisonous gas encountered in coal mines and made up chiefly of carbon monoxide.

Hence, the correct option is (D).

64. The shot firer shall carefully test for inflammable gas at all places within a radius of 18 m of the place of firing.

A Shotfirer must be appointed by the Quarry Operator and hold a current registration card to carry out shot firing operations issued by SOLAS or approved by a body in another Member State of the European Communities recognised by SOLAS as equivalent to the FETAC award under the Scheme or an award approved by a body in a state other than a Member State and recognised by SOLAS as equivalent to the award.

Only a Shotfirer or a trainee Shotfirer appointed by the Operator and under the close personal supervision of a Shotfirer may carry out shot firing operations.

Regulation 49 of the Safety, Health and Welfare at Work (Quarries) Regulations, 2008 require the shot firer in conjunction with the explosives supervisor to carry out any shot firing operations in accordance with the shot firing rules and blast specification.

Hence, the correct option is (B).

65. Modern flame safety lamps can withstand an air velocity of 15 m/s.

Safety lamp, lighting device used in places, such as mines, in which there is danger from the explosion of flammable gas or dust.

Hence, the correct option is (C).

66. Chromatography is an analytical technique commonly used for separating a mixture of chemical substances into its individual components so that the individual components can be thoroughly analyzed. Force is particularly important in chromatography when considering flow rate and back pressure with different column formats.

Force and pressure go hand-in-hand. There are also the intermolecular forces, such as hydrogen-bonding and dipole-dipole interactions in chromatography, The London dispersion force is a temporary attractive force that results when the electrons in two adjacent atoms occupy positions that make the atoms form temporary dipoles. This force is sometimes called an induced dipole-induced dipole attraction.

Hence, the correct option is (D).

67. The disadvantage of the coiled or helical shaped packed chromatographic column is that it cannot be repacked easily. It is compact in size and can easily be heated in an even manner.

Hence, the correct option is (B).

68. Capillary columns are constructed using fused silica. Fused quartz or fused silica is glass consisting of silica in amorphous (non-crystalline) form. It differs from traditional glasses in containing no other ingredients, which are typically added to glass to lower the melt temperature. Fused silica, therefore, has high working and melting temperatures.

Hence, the correct option is (D).

69. According to the Coal Mines Regulations, 1957, article 95A, "no road for trucks and dumper shall have a gradient steeper than at least 1 in 14 at any place".

Steep slopes are legally defined as hillsides having a 15 foot, or greater, vertical rise over 100 feet of horizontal run, or 15% slope (Figure 1). They are often undesirable ar- eas for development due to the difficulty of building on steep grades.

Hence, the correct option is (D).

70. 15m from the surface the temparature is constant.

The Earth gets hotter as one travels towards the core, known as the geothermal gradient. The geothermal gradient is the amount that the Earth's temperature increases with depth. On average, the temperature increases by about 25°C for every kilometre of depth.

Hence, the correct option is (B).

71. The mechanical ash handling system consumes less amount of power. Since the power is required by the conveyor belt to transfer the ash from the boiler furnace to the overhead bunker which is located at end of the conveyor belt. In the case of pneumatic, there is high power required to draw and blow the air at high velocities and high pressures.

Hence, the correct option is (A).

72. Cyclone separators use air to swirl around the ash that has been dispensed into them. Due to centrifugal action, heavier ash settles down, whereas lighter dust/ash particles are collected in a hopper and dumped out. The air flows in a helical pattern which makes it easy for the heavier dust particle to settle down easily without interrupting the airflow.

Hence, the correct option is (A).

73. The best extinguisher for fires due to oil is foam type.

Foam is an effective smothering agent, used for liquid fires mainly. It acts by flowing over the liquid fuel oil surface and isolating the fire from the air, also prevents re-ignition due to the foam stability.

Hence, the correct option is (B).

74. The best extinguisher for gaseous fires is a dry powder.

Dry powder fire extinguishers extinguish the fire primarily by interrupting the chemical reaction taking place and cutting off the oxygen supply. They can be used on fires involving solid combustibles, flammable liquids and electricity.

Hence, the correct option is (A).

75. The manually operated alarms should be provided near all main exits and in the natural path of escape from fire and at readily accessible points which are not likely to be obstructed by smoke. It is of utmost importance to make a suitable arrangement to protect the opening in case of a fire.

Hence, the correct option is (B).

76. Manual fire extinguisher includes portable fire extinguishers, the usual being carbon dioxide type. Sometimes buckets of water and asbestos blankets may be kept ready at all times to extinguish the fire. This equipment is useful for quenching a fire immediately on its generation.

Hence, the correct option is (A).

77. The pipes are usually provided at the centre to centre distance of 3 meters. The head actuated devices, known as the sprinkler heads are situated at regular intervals, usually 3 meters along the pipe. This arrangement is adopted for important structures such as textile mills, Paper Mills, factories, theatres, hospitals, etc.

Hence, the correct option is (C).

78. The normal cultivation operations such as tilling, ploughing is difficult in wet soils. The cultivation operation becomes impossible if the free water may rise above the surface of the land in extreme cases. Such land is called swampy land.

Hence, the correct option is (B).

79. Installation of lift irrigation system is one of the remedial measures adopted to reclaim the water-logged area and others are preventive measures which keep the land free from water-logging. It is found to be a very effective method of reclaiming water-logged land.

Hence, the correct option is (D).

80. The various factors that contribute to the rise in water table i.e. water-logging are –

- Over and intensive irrigation.
- Seepage of water through canals and adjoining high lands.
- Inadequate natural drainage and surface drainage.
- Excessive rains and submergence due to floods.
- Impervious obstruction.

Excessive pumping can lower the groundwater table, and cause wells to no longer be able to reach groundwater. So, it does not contribute to the water-logging.

Hence, the correct option is (D).

81. Nylon is the strongest of all ropes in common use. It is used for absorbing shock loads, such as when lifting or towing because it has the ability to return to its original length after being stretched. It also has good abrasion resistance and can last several times longer than natural fibres. Nylon starts burning at nearly 428 Fahrenheit temperature after attaining it's melting point.

Hence, the correct option is (C).

82. The best general-purpose rope, especially for critical uses, is made from polyester.

Polyester rope is often used for sailing applications, such as rigging. Polyester is the best all-around winner for UV stability, abrasion and rot resistance along with the cost.

Hence, the correct option is (B).

83. P.R.U. pump dust sampler uses the principle of Scattering of light.

P.R.U. the pump is a dust sampling instrument comprising a D.V.P. Mark 11 pump with a swept volume of 90 cm^3. A filter paper is inserted into a bridge behind the inlet nozzle of the pump such that a circle of 1-cm diameter of the filter paper is exposed to the dust. The dust, while passing through the filter paper, produces a stain. The optical density of the stain is determined photoelectrically in a densitometer by the light that falls upon a galvanometer. The dust particle concentration is evaluated by a calibration factor. Its main disadvantage is that it underestimates the number of fine particles.

Hence, the correct option is (D).

84. The mostly used blade type in the centrifugal fan is backward. Generally, centrifugal fans have three types of blades: forward blade, backward blade, and radial blade. For both radial and forward-facing blades, the power is rising monotonically as the flow rate is increased. In the case of backward-facing blades, the maximum efficiency occurs in the region of maximum power.

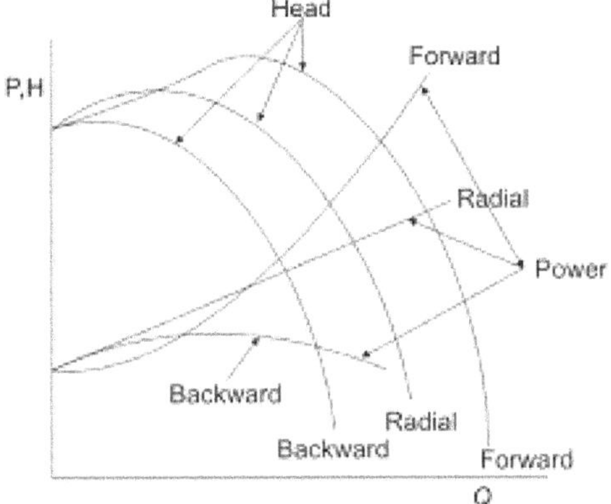

The x-axis is discharged (Q) and the y-axis is power (P) or head (H).

In the given graph, at the constant head, the power consumption is decreasing for the backward blades as the discharge is increasing whereas power consumption is increasing for radial and forward blades with increasing discharge. So, we can say that backward blades are more efficient and widely used.

Hence, the correct option is (A).

85. Konimeter dust sampler uses the principle of Impingement i.e. inertia precipitation.

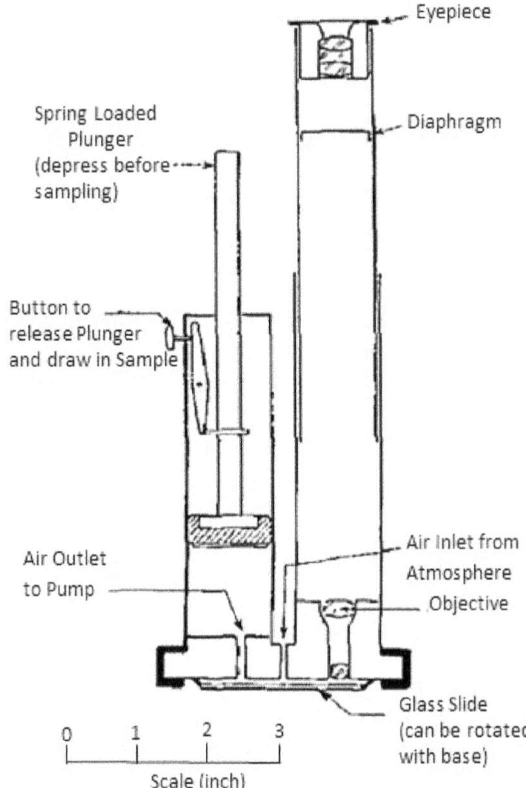

The accurate assessment of dust concentrations in relation to the health of personnel in mines is beset with difficulties. First, the fact that physiological consequences develop very slowly is compounded by dust concentrations varying across wide limits with respect to both time and place in a mine.

Hence, the correct option is (C).

86. An industrial unit which offers its entire production for export is called EPZ.

Export processing zones (EPZs) are areas within developing countries that offer incentives and a barrier-free environment to promote economic growth by attracting foreign investment for export-oriented production.

Export Oriented Units (EOU) scheme aims to increase exports from India, thereby increase foreign exchange earnings and create employment. This scheme also complements other schemes such as Free Trade Zone (FTZ) and Export Processing Zone (EPZ).

Foreign-Trade Zones (FTZ) are secure areas under U.S. Customs and Border Protection (CBP) supervision that are generally considered outside CBP territory upon activation. Located in or near CBP ports of entry, they are the United States' version of what is known internationally as free-trade zones.

Hence, the correct option is (C).

87. Crater wear is predominant in tungsten carbide tools. Crater wear happens on the tool face at a short distance from the cutting edge by the action of chip flow over the face at very high temperature. The crater wear is mainly due to diffusion and abrasion. They are commonly observed where the continuous chip is formed (usually in the ductile material).

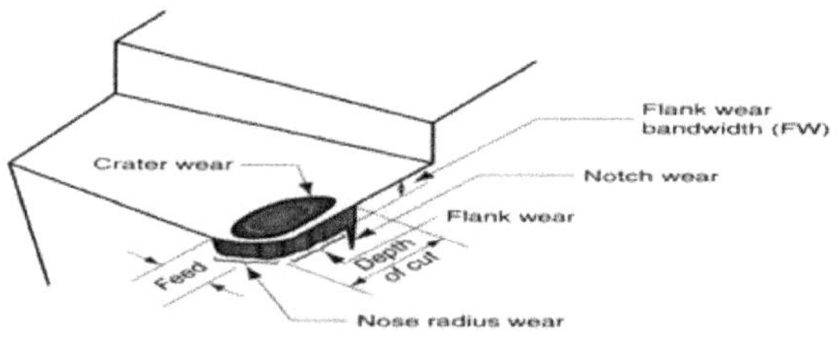

Figure - Diagram of worn cutting tool, showing the principal locations and types of wear that occur

Hence, the correct option is (B).

88. A triac (triode for alternating current (AC); also bidirectional triode thyristor or bilateral triode thyristor) is a three-terminal electronic component that conducts current in either direction when triggered. Triacs are electronic components that are widely used in AC power control applications. They are able to switch high voltages and high levels of current, and over both parts of an AC waveform.

Hence, the correct option is (D).

89. Thyristors and triacs can be triggered by a single pulse, a train of pulses or a steady d.c. voltage on the gate. Pulse triggering is most frequently used; single-pulse triggering is used in specific applications and low-cost systems, and d.c. triggering only in cases of difficulty in reaching latching current. A thyristor or triac with the anode positive with respect to the cathode, and with adequate gate drive, will turn on within 10μs. Conduction will continue irrespective of load current for as long as the gate drive is present. Conduction will continue after the gate drive ceases only if the load current has reached the latching level.

Hence, the correct option is (A).

90. For very high-speed ratio the indispensable drive is Rope Drive.

A rope drive is a form of belt drive, used for mechanical power transmission. Rope drives use a number of circular section ropes, rather than a single flat or vee belt.

Hence, the correct option is (B).

91. 15 minute rated motors are suitable for light-duty cranes. Light crane systems offer versatile material handling solutions with an ergonomic and efficient workflow. It reduces fatigue in handling and enhances productivity. Light crane systems are the best option for tasks that require precision in small spaces, where a stable lifting capacity is necessary.

Hence, the correct option is (A).

92. For medium-duty cranes, the short time rating motor used is 30 minutes.

Medium duty cranes are suitable to be fitted on two – and three –axle trucks, in a variety of setups.

A short time rating of an electric motor can be defined as the extrapolated overload rating of the motor which it can supply for the specified short time without getting overheated.

Hence, the correct option is (C).

93. In order to avoid permanent sulfating of the plates in a lead-acid battery, the voltage of the lamp on usage must not be allowed to fall below 1.8 V per cell.

Sulfation occurs when a battery is deprived of a full charge, it builds up and remains on battery plates. When too much sulfation occurs, it can impede the chemical to electrical conversion and greatly impact battery performance.

To prevent sulfation when a battery is stored, even if it's stored at a full charge, a battery must be charged enough to prevent it from dropping below 12.4 volts. Applying this maintenance charge will prevent sulfates from building up. It's also important to note that while we mentioned a battery shouldn't be stored in temperatures above 75 degrees, for every 10 degrees above room temperature, the rate of self-discharge doubles.

Hence, the correct option is (A).

94. Electric lighting is used: -

(i) In underground mines, the lighting system shall have a mid or neutral point connected with the earth and the voltage shall not exceed 125 volts between phases.

(ii) On the surface of a mine or in an open cast mine, the voltage may be raised to 250 volts, if the neutral or the midpoint of the system is connected with the earth and the voltage between the phases do not exceed 250 volts.

Hence, the correct option is (D).

95. Static pressure is measured by U-tube.

The oldest method of measuring low pressures, the simple U-tube has much to commend it. If a U-shaped glass tube is half-filled with a liquid, e.g. water, and pressure is applied to one end of the limb, the other being open to the atmosphere, the liquid will move to balance the pressure. The weight of liquid so displaced will be proportional to the pressure applied. As the difference in height of the two columns of liquid and the density are known the pressure can be calculated.

Hence, the correct option is (D).

96. Velocity pressure is measured by a pitot tube.

Method of accurately establishing the airflow rate in a duct is by traversing the duct with a pitot-static tube connected to a precision manometer. A conveniently accessible part of the duct should be selected; preferably where there is a straight parallel section of the duct of at least 5 diameters downstream of any bend, obstruction or an abrupt change of section.

Hence, the correct option is (D).

97. Manufacturing Resource Planning (MRP II) is an integrated information system used by businesses. Manufacturing Resource Planning (MRP II) evolved from early Materials Requirement Planning (MRP) systems by including the integration of additional data, such as employee and financial needs.

Hence, the correct option is (B).

98. Predetermined motion time systems (PMTS) are work measurement systems based on the analysis of work into basic human movements, classified according to the nature of each movement and the conditions under which it is made. Tables of data provide a time, at a defined rate of working, for each classification of each movement.

The first PMTS (since designated as "first-level" systems) were designed to provide times for detailed manual work and thus consisted of fundamental movements (reach, grasp, move, etc) and associated times.

Hence, the correct option is (D).

99. The maximum working hours in a day is 9.

As per the Factories Act 1948, every adult (a person who has completed 18 years of age) cannot work for more than 48 hours in a week and not more than 9 hours in a day. According to Section 51 of the Act, the spread over should not exceed 10-1/2 hours.

Hence, the correct option is (C).

100. The method of stoping best suited to low-grade deposits of horizontal or mild dip and of thickness up to 5m is called Breast stoping. Breast stoping is a method used in horizontal or near-horizontal ore bodies, where gravity is not used to move the ore around. Breast stoping lacks the characteristic "steps" of either underhand or overhand stoping, being mined in a singular cut. Room and pillar is a type of breast stoping.

Hence, the correct option is (B).

// Notes //

// Notes //

www.ingramcontent.com/pod-product-compliance
Ingram Content Group UK Ltd.
Pitfield, Milton Keynes, MK11 3LW, UK
UKHW061705190726
13853UKWH00008B/2408

9 789390 893775